CONTEMPORARY INDIGENOUS PLAYS

Bitin' Back Vivienne Cleven
Black Medea Wesley Enoch
King Hit David Milroy & Geoffrey Narkle
Rainbow's End Jane Harrison
Windmill Baby David Milroy

Introduced by Larissa Behrendt

Currency Press, Sydney

CURRENCY PLAYS

First published in 2007
by Currency Press Pty Ltd,
Gadigal Land, Suite 310, 46-56 Kippax Street, Surry Hills NSW 2010, Australia
enquiries@currency.com.au
www.currency.com.au

Reprinted 2008, 2009, 2012, 2013, 2015, 2017, 2018, 2020, 2021, 2022

Introduction © Larissa Behrendt, 2007; *Bitin' Back* © Vivienne Cleven, 2007; *Black Medea* © Wesley Enoch, 2005, 2007; *King Hit* © David Milroy and The Estate of Geoffrey Narkle, 2007; *Rainbow's End* © Jane Harrison, 2007; *Windmill Baby* © David Milroy, 2007.

COPYING FOR EDUCATIONAL PURPOSES

The Australian *Copyright Act 1968* (Act) allows a maximum of one chapter or 10% of this book, whichever is the greater, to be copied by any educational institution for its educational purposes provided that that educational institution (or the body that administers it) has given a remuneration notice to Copyright Agency (CA) under the Act.

For details of the CAL licence for educational institutions contact CA, 11/66 Goulburn Street, Sydney, NSW, 2000; tel: within Australia 1800 066 844 toll free; outside Australia 61 2 9394 7600; fax: 61 2 9394 7601; email: memberservices@copyright.com.au

COPYING FOR OTHER PURPOSES

Except as permitted under the Act, for example a fair dealing for the purposes of study, research, criticism or review, no part of this book may be reproduced, stored in a retrieval system, or transmitted in any form or by any means without prior written permission. All inquiries should be made to the publisher at the address above.

Any performance or public reading of *Bitin' Back*, *Black Medea*, *King Hit*, *Rainbow's End* or *Windmill Baby* is forbidden unless a licence has been received from the author or the author's agent. The purchase of this book in no way gives the purchaser the right to perform the play in public, whether by means of a staged production or reading. All applications for public performance should be addressed to Currency Press.

In accordance with the requirement of the Australian Media, Entertainment and Arts Alliance, Currency Press has made every effort to identify, and gain the permission of, the artists who appear in the photographs which illustrate these plays.

NATIONAL LIBRARY OF AUSTRALIA CIP DATA

Contemporary indigenous plays.
ISBN 978 0 86819 795 1.
1. Australian drama – Aboriginal Australian authors.
I. Cleven, Vivienne, 1968–. II. Behrendt, Larissa.
A822.408089915

Publication of this title was assisted by the Commonwealth Government through the Australia Council, its arts funding and advisory body.

Typeset by Dean Nottle.
Cover design by Kate Florance, Currency Press.
Jane Harrison photo by Helga Leunig.
The front cover features *Falling Star I*, a 1997 screenprint by Jimmy Pike. (Courtesy of Pat Lowe. Source: The Australian Art Print Network, www.aboriginalartprints.com.au)

Contents

vii	INTRODUCTION	
	Larissa Behrendt	
1	BITIN' BACK	
	Vivienne Cleven	
55	BLACK MEDEA	
	Wesley Enoch	
83	KING HIT	
	David Milroy and Geoffrey Narkle	
117	RAINBOW'S END	
	Jane Harrison	
201	WINDMILL BABY	
	David Milroy	

Currency Press acknowledges the Traditional Owners of the Country on which we live and work. W pay our respects to all Aboriginal and Torres Strait Islander Elders, past and present.

'This is a falling star, a true story. When I was a little boy, I was walking, walking at night-time. I was walking across to some people, and the star hit me. Then they picked me up, and my grandfather fixed me, fixed my head, after that star hit me. So I draw that star in the sky, and then it starts moving around in the sky. Then I draw the star travelling, falling towards me. Then it hit me.'

Jimmy Pike, on Falling Star I

Introduction

Larissa Behrendt

Wesley Enoch has described how he sees Indigenous performance: 'Every new work, every artist, each endeavour, is a small stone building on the one before.' There is a strong belief in interconnectedness in Aboriginal culture that reinforces an understanding that we are each inter-related to each other and our environment, and it teaches us that we stand on the shoulders of our ancestors. While contemporary Indigenous cultures are often portrayed as being eroded or diluted, these cultural values and this tradition remain strong.

Contemporary Aboriginal cultures across the country are a complex mix of diversity and shared experience. Shaped by distinctive environments, there are many shared values and, in colonial Australia, there are also many impacts of colonisation—dispossession, child-removal policies, forced assimilation, systemic racism and cyclical poverty have all left their stamp on Indigenous families and communities. These same communities also exhibit a resistance and resilience that is the hallmark of survival under the oppressive power of colonisation. It is little wonder that they recur as themes in Aboriginal storytelling, whether oral or written.

This collection of plays—each groundbreaking and significant in their own way—showcases the talent of Indigenous playwrights in capturing human experiences within circumstances where there is the scarring of struggle and hardship but also the healing of the strength of family, the warmth of love and the use of humour.

Each story introduces the audience to a gathering of strong, complex and rich characters who are sometimes iconic, sometimes archetypal, sometimes unconventional and always unique. Through each of these personalities, their experiences and their relationships, the storytellers who have created them craft stories which may be about personal and intimate interactions but are not just moving tales about life stories;

they are also stories that speak to the audience about the politics that inevitably underlies the experiences of Aboriginal people in a colonial world.

By telling stories about the complexities of family dynamics, interaction with the wider world, crushed hopes and the pursuit of dreams, personal experiences become a way of pointing to the wider political themes that define Indigenous aspirations to equality, opportunity and self-determination. Each story, as it unfolds, reaffirms the life experience of many Aboriginal people who have not been able to give voice to what they have lived through, or reminds others of the stories they have heard from parents, grandparents, aunts and uncles, especially when venturing into the autobiographical. But these stories—at the same time both universal and unique—assist in explaining distinctive Aboriginal experiences in terms that a non-Aboriginal audience can understand.

Bitin' Back is Vivienne Cleven's adaptation of her award-winning novel for the stage. Winning first the prestigious David Unaipon Award for her unpublished manuscript and then being shortlisted for the *Courier-Mail* Book of the Year Award, Cleven arrived on the literary stage with impact. In *Bitin' Back*, Cleven uses humour and mystery to explore the issues of racism and gossip in a small town as it tells the story of Mavis, a mother who hopes for a better life for her son, Nevil, through the promise of a football career. Both Nevil's cross-dressing and his own dream to become a writer challenge her plans. Reconciliation between the pair comes only after a series of comic misunderstandings and painful, sometimes violent, attempted interventions. Along the way, the audience is challenged by the fluidity and intersections of identity and sexuality as well as confronted by the subtle and overt racial tensions in a small community.

There is nothing subtle about the brutality that confronts the audience in Wesley Enoch's *Black Medea*. It captures the complex and confronting issues of violence within relationships in Aboriginal families. While this is a story with particularly Indigenous themes, Enoch's brilliant and inspired way of framing the narrative in a reinterpretation of the Greek tragedy by Euripides gives the story its universality. It explores the dark themes of revenge, sacrifice and murder. It is a compelling yet cruel tale that by standing in such stark contrast to Enoch's more feelgood, uplifting work, such as directing the popular *The Sapphires*, illustrates his range, accomplishment and stature as one of Indigenous Australia's greatest figures in the theatre.

King Hit, co-written with theatre powerhouse David Milroy, is the mesmerising tale of Geoffrey Narkle's life. It is a brave and unflinching account of a Noongar man's path from a childhood on the mission to adulthood in a travelling boxing troupe, from self-destruction and despair to inner strength, determination and survival. It is a story of the reconciliation that comes from finding peace within one's self, and of discovering solace and contentment upon understanding one's place in the world. Not only was this a cathartic story for Narkle, it became a landmark in Indigenous theatre, inspiring a generation of Aboriginal actors.

Jane Harrison's talent was evident in her first play: the phenomenally successful and politically significant *Stolen*. This collection contains her work *Rainbow's End*, which takes place in 1950s rural Victoria and is the story of three generations of women who each deal with their own challenges—overcoming past disappointment, finding one's own voice and compromise between dreams of a better life, and ties to family and country. This is ultimately a heart-warming story even though it is set against the dramatic themes of the humiliation of poverty, the brutality of violence and the crushing impacts of racism. It is through humour, strength of character and the healing power of love that hope and optimism triumph over adversity and oppression. While this is a story defined by Indigenous disadvantage, it is also a story about the relationships between mothers and daughters. For as much as it explores universal political themes, it also explores the intimate relationships that nurture the heart.

Aboriginal plays have given birth to many strong female characters. David Milroy's powerful and moving—and award-winning—*Windmill Baby* brings to life Maymay, whose lyrical voice is that of a true storyteller. With the feel of a campfire yarn, she takes the audience for a trip over the stony territory of love and loss. Set in a Kimberley cattle station and evoking memorable and provocative characters that are eccentric and endearing, *Windmill Baby* chronicles the cruelty of colonisation whilst paying tribute to the way in which wit, music and steely resolve allow Aboriginal people to survive heartbreaking events.

It won the Patrick White Award, Milroy being the first Aboriginal writer to receive this accolade, and was described by the judges as 'hard as quartz, sadly poignant and hilarious all on the one page'.

This collection of plays is not only a showcase of some of the most important moments in Indigenous theatre in the last decade. Between them, these plays encompass a cross-section of the themes that make Indigenous theatre distinctive: the experiences of forced separation, racism in the provision of everyday services, the struggle with identity, the need to reconnect to family and country, the struggle with abject poverty, the desire for self-determination and the strong ties of family, kinship and community.

But it is also a reminder of the strength of contemporary Aboriginal cultures, a continuation of the tradition of storytelling in our communities as a way of teaching, as a way of retaining history and as a way of communicating across time. Aboriginal and Torres Strait Islander cultures have an oral tradition and it is often said that this is in stark contrast to the Western tradition of valuing the written over the spoken.

But this distinction is not as simple as it is often portrayed. As this collection shows, the tradition of storytelling is powerfully alive and potently well in Indigenous Australia. And it also shows that this tradition finds itself as much in the performance and the oral telling of the story and it finds itself in the written word, the activity of playwriting. Indigenous playwrights continue this condition and this collection pulls together a powerful sample of their craft. Each play is a durable, resilient stone that both builds upon Indigenous traditions but also lays the foundation for the generations that will follow.

November 2006

Larissa Behrendt is Eualeyai/Kamillaroi woman, Professor of Law and Director of Research at the University of Technology, Sydney. She is on the Board of the Bangarra Dance Theatre, a Director of the Sydney Writers' Festival and a Board member of the Museum of Contemporary Art. Larissa's first novel, *Home*, won the David Unaipon Award.

Bitin' Back

Vivienne Cleven

Vivienne Cleven was born in 1968 and grew up in western Queensland, homeland of her Aboriginal heritage. She left school at the age of thirteen to work with her father as a jillaroo: building fences, mustering cattle, and working at various jobs on stations throughout Queensland and New South Wales. In 2000, with the manuscript *Bitin' Back*, Vivienne Cleven entered and won the David Unaipon Award. Published the following year, *Bitin' Back* was shortlisted in the 2002 *Courier-Mail* Book of the Year Award and in the 2002 South Australian Premier's Award for Fiction. She later wrote the stage adaptation of her book, which was produced by Brisbane's Kooemba Jdarra Indigenous Theatre Company. Vivienne's next novel, *Her Sister's Eye*, was published in 2002 and won the Victorian Premier's Literary Award in 2004 (Indigenous category). Both novels were also awarded the Kate Challis Raka Award for Fiction in 2006.

Roxanne McDonald as Mavis in the publicity image for the Kooemba Jdarra production of BITIN' BACK, 2005.
(Design: Jodi Edwards, Creative Plantation)

FIRST PERFORMANCE

Bitin' Back was first produced by Kooemba Jdarra Theatre Company at the Cremorne Theatre, Queensland Performing Arts Centre, Brisbane, on 5 July 2005, with the following cast:

MAVIS DOOLEY	Roxanne McDonald
BOOTY DOOLEY	Lafe Charlton
NEVIL DOOLEY	Jorde Lenoy
DARRYL KANE / ISAAC EDGE	Mark Conaghan
DOROTHY REEDMAN	Andrea Moore
DETECTIVE LYLE GOULD / MAD DOG	Hayden Spencer
MAX / MRS WARBY	Scott Witt
GRACIE	Paula Nazarski

Director, Wesley Enoch
Dramaturg, Peter Matheson
Designer, Jonathon Oxlade
Lighting Designer, David Murray
Sound Designer, Brett Collery

AUTHOR'S NOTE

The premiere production of *Bitin' Back* involved many people and thanks must go to the fabulous and incredibly talented cast who made the play a truly funny, rollercoaster of a ride—Roxanne McDonald, Jorde Lenoy, Scott Witt, Andrea Moore, Paula Narzaski, Lafe Charlton, Mark Conoghan and Hayden Spencer.

Throughout the three-year process of adapting my novel, *Bitin' Back*, I was lucky enough to have the wonderful Peter Matheson as my dramaturg. I am thankful for his support and encouragement.

A special thanks must go to Nadine McDonald-Dowd and Vera Ding (formerly of Kooemba Jdarra) who first commissioned me to write the play.

Thanks to the National Playwrights' Centre for inviting *Bitin' Back* to attend the Centre and to have the opportunity for further development.

Thank you to *Bitin' Back*'s producer Kooemba Jdarra, director Wesley Enoch, Production Designer Jonathan Oxlade, Lighting Designer David Murray, Sound Designer Brett Collery and Production Manager Abbie Trott.

Vivienne Cleven

CHARACTERS

MAVIS DOOLEY, murri, forties, confident, not easily intimidated
NEVIL DOOLEY, murri, twenty, has a macho demeanour, sensitive, intelligent
BOOTY DOOLEY, murri, forty, loud, aggressive persona
GRACIE, murri, twenty, hyperactive, suspicious, erratic, stoned most times
TREVOR DAVIDSON, white, thirty, very 'city', has the tendency to come across as 'nerdy'
GWEN HINCH, murri, forty, scatty, vulnerable
IVY WARBY, white, sixty, has an air of religious fanaticism, unpredictable, eccentric
DOROTHY REEDMAN, white, forty, dress-style evocative of the sixties, tacky, shrilly, mean-spirited
DETECTIVE LYLE GOULD, a humourless, know-all bully, narcotics cop from Brisbane
MAX BROWN, white, forty, Mandamooka's clumsy copper who tries hard to uphold an air of competent authority
ISAAC EDGE, white, thirty, dodgy drug dealer
DARRYL KANE, white, thirty, a full-of-himself, strutting Casanova
MAD DOG, punch-drunk pugilist

SETTING

Mandamooka, a dusty bush town somewhere west of Brisbane. The action takes place in Mavis's kitchen.

A NOTE ON LANGUAGE

The language of the play is a mixture of Standard English and Aboriginal English, and is significant to the characters of the piece.

ACT ONE

SCENE ONE

Time: The present. Afternoon.

Place: Mandamooka football field.

MAVIS, BOOTY, GRACIE, MAX *(in uniform)*, DOROTHY, DARRYL *and* MRS WARBY *wait for the game to begin. Some supporters carry home-made signs with the words: 'The Blackouts'. Others wear the team colours of black and orange on scarves and beanies.*

A whistle blows. NEVIL *enters. He runs past, football in hand. He holds the ball up to the* CROWD *who jump, clap, cheer.*

CROWD: Onya, Nev! Yahoo, the Blackouts!

MAVIS: Go, son, goal for Mum!

> MRS WARBY *moves through the* CROWD *shaking an ice-cream container and an uncooked chicken at everyone. Hanging from her neck is a pair of binoculars and slung over her shoulder is a duffle bag.*

MRS WARBY: Tickets here! Everyone, dig deep for the church! The reverend needs our help! The new church pew won't build itself!

> NEVIL *sprints by, dodging, weaving and ducking.*

MAVIS: [*to the audience*] That's me boy there. He's the star player for Mandamooka's footy team, the Blackouts. He loves footy. It's his life. His future.

> *The* CROWD*'s more excited now, waving signs, scarves.*

CROWD: Score for Mooka! Go the Blackouts!

BOOTY: Nevil, don't arse around! You can do better than that!

> *Distracted,* NEVIL *drops the ball. The* CROWD *moans, disappointed.*

DOROTHY: Get the bloody ball, Dooley! Move your useless arse!

> DARRYL *struts across to* GWEN, *whispers something, gesturing wildly with his hands.* GWEN *turns to him, looking annoyed, then*

shuts him up with a kiss on the lips. BOOTY *gallops down the sideline, arms flailing.*

BOOTY: Fuck me roan, Nevil! Stop playin' like a nancy!

    MAVIS *points to* BOOTY.

MAVIS: [*to the audience*] That's his Uncle Booty. He's just too hard on Nevil sometimes. God knows, Nevil tries like hell to please him. But a woman knows where it all comes from…

BOOTY: Don't be a pussy, Nevil! Move faster, stop bein' a fucken sheila!

    NEVIL *picks up the ball and tears towards the finish line.* MRS WARBY *shakes the container harder, more frantic.*

MRS WARBY: Support the church! We need that pew! Someone buy a ticket, for God's sake!

MAVIS: [*to the audience*] Booty was Nevil's age when he was picked by the state reps to play, but things went wrong. Someone lied—Dottie Reedman's mother. She hated the fact that Booty was better than her kid. Couldn't stand the idea of Booty being picked! Womba.

    NEVIL'*s closer to the goalpost now.*

CROWD: Go, Nevil, go! Goal! Yahooo!

BOOTY: That's the way, boy! Show us what ya made of!

MAVIS: [*to the audience*] Soon Dottie's mother started to gossip. Word reached the selectors that Booty loved the grog too much. They said they didn't want a drunk on the team. It was all bulldust. Booty's once-in-a-lifetime chance was ruined by a lie! I hate lies! I hate liars even more!

CROWD: The Blackouts are better than the rest 'cause they're the best!

BOOTY: Dodge him, Nevil! Hook left!

    MRS WARBY *shakes the container even harder.*

MRS WARBY: First prize, a roast chook! One of my own hens! Golden. Crisp. Juicy!

MAVIS: That's what worries me about Nevil, how others'll treat him. I know how much damage gossip and lies cause. In this town, that's part and parcel of life. Way the dice rolls round here. Makes a woman sick.

    NEVIL *tears past, faster. The goalposts are closer. The* CROWD *builds in excitement.* NEVIL *scores! The* CROWD *goes wild and mobs* NEVIL, *all praising him at once: 'Good game', 'You're our star'. They jostle each other to get closer to him.* BOOTY *cuts through the* CROWD *and grabs him in a bear hug.*

   MRS WARBY *reaches into the container and pulls out a ticket.*

MRS WARBY: Mavis Dooley! God bless you, Mavis. You'll be in the reverend's prayers tonight.

   MRS WARBY *hands* MAVIS *the chicken.*

MAVIS: Thanks, Mrs Warby. I'll share this with the team later.

   NEVIL *holds the football in the air, a salute.*

BOOTY: No doubt about it, you're too deadly, Nevil!

MAVIS: You gotta love him. A good kid. [*To the audience*] He's the best player in Mandamooka. Football's everythin' to him. And it'll be over me dead carcass if I let any bastard in this town bring him down the way they did Booty. Been there, seen that, run the miles.

   MAX *slaps* NEVIL *affectionately on the back.*

MAX: Well done, son! You do Mandamooka proud!

   MAX*'s walkie-talkie kicks into life. He unhooks it from his belt, speaks.*

[*Into the walkie-talkie*] Max here.

   LYLE GOULD*'s voice crackles over the air.*

LYLE: [*voice-over*] Max, Isaac Edge alert. He's in your area somewhere, suspected of carrying skag. On your toes, cowboy. Over.

MAX: [*into the walkie-talike*] Right to it, Lyle. Over and out.

   MAX *fumbles to hook the walkie-talkie back on his belt. He looks around, taking in the* CROWD. DARRYL *gestures to* GWEN.

DARRYL: Here, take this!

   DARRYL *stuffs a drug bag into* GWEN*'s Avon bag.*

GWEN: Darryl, what are you—?! Christ's sakes! Watch my Avon!

DARRYL: Shut the fuck up and hold onto it!

   DARRYL *exits.*

GWEN: Darryl, Darryl, where ya goin', Darryl? [*To* MAVIS] See you later, Mave!

   NEVIL, BOOTY, GRACIE, GWEN, MAX *and* DARRYL *all exit.* MRS WARBY *moves across to* MAVIS. DOROTHY *rushes over to* MRS WARBY. *She spots* MAVIS, *stops flat and glares at her.*

MAVIS: What are you gawkin' at, Reedman?
DOROTHY: It isn't a pretty picture, that's for sure!
MAVIS: Oh, looked in the mirror lately?
DOROTHY: Rumour has it, Nevil's burnt out! Losing it big time. Just look at the way he dropped that ball, says it all.
MAVIS: That was an accident!
DOROTHY: Just admit it, Dooley, your kid can't play! Shit, I doubt if he could even play with himself!
MAVIS: You're just like that lying mother of yours, Reedman! My Nevil's the best player, full stop! Burnt out! What, you couldn't think of a better lie?!
DOROTHY: Don't you call me a liar! My mother told the truth for what it was—Booty was a drunken, talentless loser! Still is!
MRS WARBY: Settle down, Dorothy. No arguments today! Please.
MAVIS: Your mother saw sweet f-all! She couldn't tell the truth if it bit her on the arse!
DOROTHY: Shut up, Dooley! I don't give a hot piss what you think!
MRS WARBY: Lord, oh Lord. Not this again!
MAVIS: Booty would have had a chance if Rita hadn't ruined it with her lies!
MRS WARBY: I thought this nonsense was finished years ago.
DOROTHY: Nothing good will ever come of Nevil! He'll wind up just like his uncle.
MRS WARBY: Enough, Dorothy! Be pleasant. No more fights. Let's move on. Good. Now, I've some important news for you both. I heard on the grapevine that the footy selectors from Brissie are in.
DOROTHY & MAVIS: [*together*] They are?!
MRS WARBY: They'll only be here for a few days. Nevil and Jerry better get their acts together. They only want one player.
DOROTHY: They'll pick my Jerry!
MAVIS: Nevil!
DOROTHY: Jerry!
MAVIS: Nevil!

MRS WARBY *looks at both women in turn.*

MRS WARBY: Nevil or Jerry, that's the big question, isn't it?
DOROTHY: Jerry's always been a great player. The best in Mandamooka. Even the coach reckons so.
MAVIS: Oh, that's shit! Nevil's the only star round here! He'll be picked.

MRS WARBY: Now, now, ladies, both boys are top players.
DOROTHY: Jerry's top-grade! They'll pick him, that's that!
MAVIS: Don't bet on it, Reedman!
DOROTHY: Your kid's a real queer bird. Six-pack short of a carton.
MRS WARBY: Good Lord, Dorothy! Every time you use such vulgarisms, the Lord weeps. Upon my soul, he does.
MAVIS: Leave my boy alone! Oh, just shut ya guts, Reedman!
DOROTHY: Screw you, Dooley! You'll get yours one day, bitch!

    DOROTHY *exits*.

MAVIS: What's bitin' that cow?
MRS WARBY: Most likely the Devil. Oh, and Mavis, I've a little something for you. I made these this morning.

    MRS WARBY *pulls out a tray of lamingtons from her handbag and gives them to* MAVIS.

MAVIS: Mrs Warby, you really shouldn't have. Proper thoughtful of ya, but. Thanks.
MRS WARBY: Say, Mavis, hate to be a stickybeak but I saw a woman in your yard this morning. Pretty little thing, except for those muscular arms. Almost jumped the fence.
MAVIS: Probably Nev's girl, Gracie.
MRS WARBY: By George, such big shoulders! Footballer shoulders, in fact.
MAVIS: Mrs Warby, I gotta go now. Have to keep Nevil on his toes, 'specially since the selectors will pick him. A woman has to make sure he's ready!

    MAVIS *exits*.

◆ ◆ ◆ ◆ ◆

SCENE TWO

Later. Kitchen / backyard.

In the background are a couple of rusting kerosene drums housing straggly geraniums. On the other side is a clothes line, clothes already pegged—bloomers, a dress. A dish of water and a dog chain lie nearby.

In the foreground is the kitchen. The room is spotlessly clean with an old table and worn chairs in the centre. A stack of plates, a kettle, enamel tea mugs and various other kitchen items are placed on a sideboard. Some pots and a phone hang from the wall. A broom and mop are in the corner. Against the wall is a rusting fridge and taking pride of place on the door is a huge football poster. An assortment of football paraphernalia—trophies, medals, ribbons—decorate the room.

MAVIS *is busy unpacking lamingtons into a huge container overpacked with them.*

MAVIS: [*to herself*] Bloody gossipers! That lying cow Reedman! Why do people have to lie?

> NEVIL *enters, dressed in his football clothes. He grabs something to eat from the fridge, then kisses his mother.* MAVIS *squashes a lamington angrily into the container.* NEVIL *exits.*

What good does it do to tell lies?! Only causes—

> *Hearing a noise, she looks behind.*

Only causes grief. This town. This spiteful bloody town.

> NEVIL *enters again. He's dressed in an oversized frock, face made up, clutching a handbag. He glances at his mother, straightens his hem. He dares to go closer to her.*

I hate liars! Turns me gut!

> MAVIS *slams the container hard on the table. Surprised,* NEVIL *jumps back.*

So many lamingtons! What's a woman to do with them all? That Dorothy Reedman! She can get ripped!

> *She picks up a lamington, shakes it. Hearing a small noise from behind, she spins around to face* NEVIL. *At first, she's not sure what she's looking at. A woman: who? A thing: what?*

NEVIL: Hey, Mum. Do you reckon you can take up the hem?

> *The container of lamingtons falls to the floor.*

MAVIS: Huh?
NEVIL: The hem. [*Indicating the dress*] Can you take up the hem?
MAVIS: Nev? Nevil, that you?

NEVIL smoothes down his frock.

NEVIL: From now on you have to call me Jean.
MAVIS: What?
NEVIL: Call me Jean. Jean Rhys.
MAVIS: Jesus, what the f-ing hell are ya coming at?! Something wrong with ya, Nevil?

She moves closer to him, inspecting his face.

NEVIL: No.
MAVIS: Oh, I get it! A joke. A laugh on Mum. Real funny!
NEVIL: No joke. I'm serious. Dead serious.

MAVIS reaches into her bra and pulls out a hanky. She swipes at his face with it.

MAVIS: Just take a look at yourself. Such disgrace! Get that eyeshada off right this minute! Me good Avon too!
NEVIL: You don't understand. It's not what you think.
MAVIS: Enough tomfoolery! Outta that frock. The footy selectors are in town! Yeah, you heard me, the selectors! You need to get over to the clubhouse right away!
NEVIL: Stuff the clubhouse!
MAVIS: You miss ya father, that it? You can talk to me about it, Nevil. Thing is, love, he was a stinkin' bludger. We're better off without him.
NEVIL: It's got nothing to do with Dad!
MAVIS: Well, it must be those mates of yours. Feedin' ya maryjawana. Now you're all headcracked on it.
NEVIL: No! It's not like that! Just listen—
MAVIS: Enough arsein' around, Nevil. Take my bloody good bingo frock off. Right now!

MAVIS tries to tear the dress off him. NEVIL backs away, holding tight his dress.

NEVIL: No! No, don't rip the dress! Please, Mum, I just wanna tell you—
MAVIS: Go get dressed proper. Leave me frocks alone! What's Gracie gonna think if she sees you lookin' like some fancied-up trollop?
NEVIL: Ah, what's the point?

NEVIL exits.

MAVIS: [*to the audience*] Christ, can you wake up gay? Must do, Nevil did. Geez, woman'll have to get his Uncle Booty over to have a man talk to him.

Later. The kitchen.

MAVIS *and* BOOTY *are at the table, drinking tea, eating lamingtons.*

He wasn't like that yesterday. Maybe he's, he's gorn all man mad, you know what I'm talkin'. Yeah, gay. A lesbian now.

BOOTY: All this tryin' to be a poofter. Fuck me roan, what's a man to do? I've seen this sorta shit on *Ricki Lake*. That's where these ideas come from—TV!

MAVIS: Maybe it's those books brainwashin' him. Givin' him certain womba ideas. Woman should take him to Dr Chin's clinic.

BOOTY: We can't let him outside in that frock, Mave. Footy team'd tear him apart!

MAVIS: It's not only that either… Reckons to call himself Jean Ree, Ri, Rice… Oh, some fancy-arse name. Where the hell did he come up with that?

BOOTY: Don't shake my ring to find the answer. Got me fried, Sis.

MAVIS: It's Nevil's no-hoper father. He's to blame. Nevil misses him. Gotta be it.

BOOTY: Bullshit! Boy's got a screw loose upstairs. This is bad fucken business, no question.

MAVIS: But what can we do?

BOOTY: Calm ya water, Mave. I'll come up with something. Find some way to sort him out.

MAVIS: Do it quick smart, Booty. He needs to be picked by those selectors. A chance at somethin' good for his future.

BOOTY *exits.*

Hope to God no one clocks the boy.

There is a knock on the door. MAVIS *jumps up, startled. She creeps to the door. There's another knock. Uncertain, she just stands there. Finally, she throws a look towards* NEVIL*'s room—all quiet. There's another knock, much louder, more forceful this time.*

Who's there?

GRACIE: It's me. Gracie. Mum, why's this door locked? Let me in!

MAVIS: Jumpin' Jesus!

    MAVIS *opens the door.* GRACIE *enters, munching on a Mars Bar.*

GRACIE: Hey, Mum. What's with you? Looks like you've seen a ghost.

MAVIS: Blood pressure, Gracie. Bad today.

GRACIE: That's shitty, huh. Where's Nevil?

MAVIS: He's, um, crook, love. Got a real bad flu and it's makin' him delirious. Boy's startin' to see things now. Actin' real womba, like.

GRACIE: Deadset. That was fast. He was okay yesterday.

MAVIS: Funny turnout.

GRACIE: Sounds dicey. I better take him to Dr Chin.

MAVIS: No! No, love, I'll look after him. He'll be full of beans again soon.

GRACIE: You'd better tell him to get his arse over to the oval, pronto. The footy selectors are already at the clubhouse. And the coach is gettin' hairy waitin' for him.

MAVIS: He'll be there. And, Gracie, if you see his team-mates, tell them not to be coming round here 'til Nev's back to himself again.

GRACIE: Gotcha, Mum. Tell Nev to get better soon.

    GRACIE *exits.*

MAVIS: [*to the audience*] Never thought I'd see the day where a woman'd have to lie. No matter which way the dice rolls, it just ain't right. This rubbish has to stop, otherwise Nevil will ruin everything. His football dream will go right down the gurgler. There's no way I can have that!

    MAVIS *exits.*

♦♦♦♦♦

SCENE THREE

MAVIS *opens a side door to reveal* NEVIL*'s bedroom. Neatly stacked books are piled everywhere, some on side tables, others in a heap on the floor. Placed nearby is an old typewriter, reams of paper alongside. The team jersey and a football lie carelessly on the floor.*

MAVIS *and* BOOTY *enter.* NEVIL *is lying back on his bed, frocked and made-up, reading* Wide Sargasso Sea *by Jean Rhys.*

BOOTY: Strike me dead! What's that shit on your dial? And what do you think you're doing in that fucken frock?!
MAVIS: What the…?! [*Snatching the novel*] So this is where all this Jean business comes from!

She gives BOOTY *the book.* BOOTY *hurls the novel across the room, goes closer to* NEVIL, *looks harder.*

NEVIL: This [*pointing to his face*] is make-up. Make-up. And call me Jean from now on. Jean Rhys.

BOOTY *grabs him in a headlock.* NEVIL *struggles madly to get away.*

Let me go!
BOOTY: That ain't gonna happen until you get ya act together!
NEVIL: Piss off!
MAVIS: Booty, here!

She tosses him a dishrag.

[*To* NEVIL] Come on, love, go get dressed proper. Quick now!

BOOTY *roughly shoves* NEVIL *around, trying to wipe the make-up off with the rag.*

BOOTY: Deadset lunacy! Get into that bathroom and clean that shit off your dial, ya ratbag!

NEVIL *pulls away.*

NEVIL: Stop it! Leave me alone!
BOOTY: Look here, son, you're gonna mess up ya chance of being picked by the selectors. What, you 'spect me and ya mother to stand by and watch you ruin everything?!
NEVIL: Listen, Uncle—
MAVIS: No, you listen, Nevil! Just hear Uncle out.
BOOTY: Sonny Jim, if you wanna have a man talk, let me know… But if you keep on with this shit, I'm gonna have to settle ya down and pretty fucken soon!

NEVIL *shrugs: whatever.*

Right then, that's that. How about a cuppa tea, Mave?

BOOTY *and* MAVIS *exit into the kitchen and sit at the table.*

Where'd he come up with this bullshit?

MAVIS: Beats me.
BOOTY: Look, Sis, I don't wanna worry ya any more, but…
MAVIS: Booty?
BOOTY: Thing is, Mave, you'd better keep ya eyes peeled. Watch the boy close. He could wind up wearing ya bloomers 'fore too long.

> NEVIL *enters, frocked, sidling along the wall, clutching his handbag.*

What the hell do ya think you're doing now?
NEVIL: Just thought that I'd—I'm going to the dole office. Got an interview.
BOOTY: You're not goin' anywhere dressed like that!
NEVIL: I've had it with you, Uncle. I'm outta here!

> MAVIS *looks at* BOOTY, *concerned.*

MAVIS: Oh, no!

> BOOTY *charges at* NEVIL, *tackling him hard to the floor.* NEVIL *thrashes wildly, trying to get away, pounding* BOOTY *on the back with the bag.*

NEVIL: Mum, get him off me!
BOOTY: Quick, Mavis, get him to his room!

> MAVIS *looks fearful, uncertain.*

MAVIS: Don't be too rough on him, Booty.

> BOOTY *drags* NEVIL *along by the handbag. He gets him to his bedroom, shoves him in and slams shut the door.* NEVIL *pounds hard on the door.*

NEVIL: Let me out! Open the door!
BOOTY: Gotta key, Mave?
MAVIS: For what?
BOOTY: We'll have to lock him away. Can't have him fancy-arsein' round in that frock. Somebody'll clock him. You can bet on it.

> NEVIL *pounds harder.*

NEVIL: Mum! Muumm! Help me, let me out!

> MAVIS *roots around in her bra and pulls out a set of door keys.*

MAVIS: Booty, you can't lock a grown man in his bedroom.

> NEVIL *sings a few bars of 'I Am Woman' by Helen Reddy.*

BOOTY: That's fucken done it! Key, Mavis.

MAVIS *reluctantly hands over the key.*

MAVIS: Is lockin' him up really gonna help?

BOOTY: He'll be back to normal tomorra. This business'll blow over soon enough. Good shake-up, that's all he needs, Mave.

BOOTY *exits.* MAVIS *stares at the door for a moment, uncertain. She places a hand on the doorknob as if to let* NEVIL *out.* NEVIL *resumes singing the song.* MAVIS *reels back from the door.*

MAVIS: Flamin' Jesus! [*To* NEVIL] You can come out when ya wake up to yourself! [*To the audience*] No wonder me blood pressure's playin' up. I don't like this. Dangerous. 'Specially in this town. Only thing a woman can do is to keep him locked away. For his own good.

◆ ◆ ◆ ◆ ◆

SCENE FOUR

MAVIS *places a variety of party foods on the kitchen table. She sets down a plate stacked mile-high with lamingtons.* GWEN *enters.*

MAVIS: Where is everyone?

GWEN *arranges her make-up on the other side of the table, tubes of lipstick, eye shadow, etc.*

GWEN: Told them all my Avon party was gonna be on today. Hope they turn up. Mave, while we've got a quiet minute, can I have a yarn to you about somethin'? There's trouble again. Darryl Kane's spreadin' even more talk about me around town.

MAVIS: I hear ya, Gwen, but I've got me own problems. Nevil with all his headcrackin' ideas. Worry, worry, that's all a woman does these days.

GWEN: Thing is, Darryl can be such a good bloke. Just wish he'd stop saying shit about me. Telling everyone I'm a slut.

MAVIS: Say, Gwen, does—you know, does your boy ever think he's—well, he's somebody else? A woman or something like that?

GWEN: Geez, no! Why, Mave, what's going down?

MAVIS: It's Nevil, he's—

DARRYL *enters, drunk, holding a bottle of rum. He staggers across to the women.*

DARRYL: Heeyy, Gwenny!

GWEN: The bloody hell's he doing here?

DARRYL: Got a coupla bucks?

GWEN: Darryl, I told you not to come here drunk! You'll fucken-well wreck my Avon party!

MAVIS: Gwen, here's ya chance to stop the rumours. Put an end to his rubbish right now!

GWEN: That's not gonna prove anything.

MAVIS: Enough is enough! Get this sorted, once and for all, Gwen.

GWEN: Not a good thing to face Darryl when he's charged-up.

MAVIS: Don't let him get away with it! He'll f-up ya good name! Ruin ya life, Avon career, everything.

DARRYL: [*to* GWEN] Fuck's going on here?

    MAVIS *shoves* GWEN *forward.*

MAVIS: Gwen's got something to say.

    DARRYL *takes a swig of rum, then wipes his mouth on his shirt sleeve.*

DARRYL: Spit it out, Gwen.

GWEN: Darryl, I don't want you spreading any more filthy talk about me. I don't like it.

DARRYL: Hold your guns, woman! What talk?

GWEN: I'm not... I'm not the town bike, Darryl. There's no need—

MAVIS: To go round tellin' everyone that she is! And, Kane, everyone knows you've been humping Gwenny behind your wife's back. Now you've the hide to say she's the town trollop!

DARRYL: What's it to do with you?

MAVIS: Let him have it, woman!

GWEN: Darryl, I... I want you to stop it. No more.

DARRYL: Shut up, Gwen. [*To* MAVIS] Mind your own fucking business!

MAVIS: Outta my house, Kane, before I sool the pig dogs onto ya! Gorn, get!

DARRYL: Oowwhh, I'm so scared. Gonna piss me pants. Shut your crack, old bag!

GWEN: Darryl! Settle down! Don't talk to my mate like that.

DARRYL: I thought I told you to keep away from the trouble-making bitch!

> DARRYL *grabs* GWEN *by the shirt collar and starts roughly pushing her around, tearing her shirt in the process.*

MAVIS: Kane, keep ya filthy paws off Gwenny!

> DARRYL *turns on* MAVIS *and fiercely knocks her to the ground. He stands over her, cracking his knuckles.*

DARRYL: Now fuck off!

> MAVIS *gets up, pats down her hair and straightens her frock.*

MAVIS: [*to the audience*] I've never been the type of woman to disgrace herself in front of others. And never been the type of person to think a dust-up'll solve anything... But today he's got on my goat good and proper!

> MAVIS *charges at* DARRYL. *She tackles him mid-section, bringing him to his knees.* DARRYL *gets shakily to his feet.*

DARRYL: Black bitch! Watch that kid of yours... little weed-eatin' bastard... one day... one day that cone-suckin' shithead might... might meet with an accident!

MAVIS: Get outta here before I set the coppers onto ya!

DARRYL: Bitch! Cow! One of these days... be real sorry...

> DARRYL *exits.*

GWEN: Thanks for looking after me, Mave.

MAVIS: No man's gonna hurt a woman in front of me. This old scrapper's been there, done that, picked up the pieces.

GWEN: Mave, Darryl never threatens anyone unless he means it. There's no telling what he'll do. Keep an eye on Nevil.

MAVIS: Darryl's just fulla hot wind. But, Gwenny, his filthy lies will wreck your life. Be the ruination of your Avon career.

> GWEN *exits.* MAVIS *sits at the kitchen table, peeling potatoes.* GRACIE *enters. She paces the kitchen, looking around suspiciously, opening cupboards, doors, etc.*

It's like I said, Gracie. Nevil's got football stress. Kickin' that ball too hard. Gone to his head. Boy's not up to seein' anyone just yet.

> GRACIE *sits down. She pulls out a Mars Bar from her pocket and eats it.*

GRACIE: It's like he's hidin' from me. And he hasn't even been over to the clubhouse yet. Everyone's askin' about him, especially the selectors.

MAVIS: The selectors?! Oh, Christ! Listen, tell them that Nevil will be there tomorrow, hail or shine.

GRACIE: There's talk that Jerry Reedman's to be selected. Dotty's there every day supporting him.

MAVIS: Love, tell those selectors that Nevil's been, um, sick. But he'll be right again soon. Dotty's there every day, Gracie?

GRACIE: First thing. Cleaning Jerry's boots, running with him round the oval, throwing the ball with him and all. He's doin' well. Everyone's real 'pressed.

MAVIS: Is that so? Well, Jerry's days are numbered. Once Nev's back on his feet again, he'll show those selectors what a real footballer is!

NEVIL is heard singing 'I Am Woman' from offstage.

GRACIE: Who's that?

MAVIS: Oh, that's Mrs Warby, the lonely old piece next door. Now, Gracie, over to the clubhouse and pass on my message.

GRACIE: Tell Nevil I'm sicka his pissin' around! Girl doesn't know what's what with him any more.

MAVIS: I hear you, love. But gorn, run along. That's the girl.

MAVIS pushes GRACIE to the door. GRACIE exits. MAVIS goes into NEVIL's bedroom. NEVIL's on his bed with a typewriter and a ream of paper.

Nevil, I've had a gutful! Put an end to this rubbish. Right then, get dressed and I'll walk you to the oval.

NEVIL: No, I don't want to. Mum, just… Oh, leave me alone already.

MAVIS: Nevil, wake up to yourself. Ya name's not Jean and you're not a white woman. You're a black man and ya name's Nevil Arthur Dooley!

NEVIL: Cool your motor.

MAVIS: You're turning me into a liar. What about Gracie? You gonna tell her what's going?

NEVIL: I never told you to lie. I'll tell Gracie when I'm ready.

MAVIS points at the typewriter.

MAVIS: What are you doing with that thing?

NEVIL: Just, just writing…
MAVIS: Writing? Writing what?!
NEVIL: Well, it's, ah, it's a story.
MAVIS: Waste of time. There's no future in writing stupid bloody stories. Now, on ya feet and off to see the coach. Quick, on the double!
NEVIL: I'm not going anywhere. Got better things to do. Important stuff to think about.
MAVIS: That's enough, Nevil. Stop talking like that.
NEVIL: Mum, there's other things in life apart from footy. Oh, why do I bother? No matter what I say, you always want things your way.
MAVIS: Football is ya way outta this town. Your future. Now, across to the clubhouse. Everyone's counting on you. Don't mess this up, Nevil.
NEVIL: Just listen to me, will you, Mum! I don't care about football. Not interested. Let them pick Jerry Reedman!

> MAVIS *reels back, hand over her heart.*

MAVIS: What?! What'd you say?
NEVIL: You heard me. Let them pick Jerry. Jerry Reedman.
MAVIS: How could you? How could you say such a shitty thing?

> BOOTY *enters.*

BOOTY: Righto, Nevil, outta that bloody sickenin' skirt. I'm takin' ya pig shooting, fella.
NEVIL: I hate shooting!
BOOTY: Get dressed!

> NEVIL *reaches for a blouse on the floor.*

Not on your life!

> BOOTY *tears the blouse from him. He pushes* NEVIL *into the bedroom.*

Fucken disgrace—your poor mother—Come on, son, for Christ's sakes—
NEVIL: It just never stops… you, Mum, this town… always telling me what to do. Jesus, I'm not a kid any more!

> BOOTY *walks back out of* NEVIL's *bedroom, smiling.*

BOOTY: All sorted, Sis. His head'll be screwed back on the right way when I'm finished with him. Fucken lunatic.

MAVIS: What if someone sees him? Woman's been lying to everyone, saying he's gone away. Only a matter of time before everyone in town'll suss the truth.
BOOTY: Just trust me on this one, Mave. I'll fix him good, you just see.
MAVIS: Be careful with him. After all, he's only just a kid.

> NEVIL *comes back into the room, dressed in jeans and T-shirt. On his feet, however, is a pair of high-heel shoes.* BOOTY *and* MAVIS *do not spot the shoes.*

BOOTY: See! What'd I tell you?

> MAVIS *follows them to the door.*

MAVIS: See ya this arvo, love!

> BOOTY *and* NEVIL *exit. Pig dogs bark.*

[*To the audience*] With Booty on the job now, things'll be right again soon.

> MRS WARBY *enters, carrying a plate of lamingtons, and her handbag over her shoulder.*

MRS WARBY: Yoo-hoo, Mavis!
MAVIS: Gee, Mrs Warby! You nearly gave a woman a heart turn!

> MRS WARBY *gives* MAVIS *the lamingtons.*

MRS WARBY: Was that Nevil? Funny thing, could have sworn I spotted him yesterday in your fancy bingo frock. Jazzed up with face paint!

> MAVIS *gives a gammon laugh.*

MAVIS: Face paint!
MRS WARBY: Something funny?
MAVIS: Oh, no, I was—
MRS WARBY: People don't usually laugh at nothing. Mavis, do be careful, don't lose yourself in the darkness. Toodeloo.

> MRS WARBY *makes her way to the exit.* TREVOR *enters, briefcase in hand. He stops, looks around as though searching for something. He goes over to* MAVIS.

TREVOR: Hi. Can you tell me where I might be able to find Nevil Dooley? I was told he lives in the area somewhere.
MAVIS: He lives here. Who are you?

> TREVOR*'s mobile phone rings. He answers it.*

TREVOR: [*into the phone*] Hello?
MAVIS: A dole officer!

> DOROTHY *enters. She stops and stares hard at* TREVOR *who is some distance away from her.*

TREVOR: [*into the phone*] Yeah, Jean Rhys, can you believe it? The genius of such a thing. These writers!

> TREVOR *places the phone back in his shirt pocket, then messes about with his briefcase.* DOROTHY *sees* MRS WARBY *about to exit.*

DOROTHY: Mrs Warby, hang on. Did you hear that?!
MRS WARBY: Hear what?

> DOROTHY *indicates* TREVOR, *then his briefcase.* MRS WARBY *peers through her binoculars at the briefcase.*

What?! Now, who?!
DOROTHY: He was saying something about Jean Reeze. Who's Jean Reeze? And just take a look at that briefcase. Remind you of something?
MRS WARBY: By gee, does ring a bell…
DOROTHY: Remember that episode of *Blue Heelers*? The bloke, that briefcase… those drugs…
MRS WARBY: Sweet Jesus! Well, I'll be…
DOROTHY: Take a closer look at him. He look like someone to you?
MRS WARBY: Oh yes, yes. Sort of resembles a younger Cary Grant.
DOROTHY: Not bloody likely. I bet that's Isaac Edge. The bloke the cops are after.
MRS WARBY: But what the daylights is he doing with Mavis?

> *The women exchange suspicious glances, whispering between themselves about drugs, the briefcase, Jean Rhys.* DOROTHY *and* MRS WARBY *exit.* TREVOR *stands before* MAVIS.

TREVOR: Oh, sorry about that. I'm Trevor Davidson. Nevil's friend. Just drove down from Brisbane and thought I'd come see him. You're his mum?
MAVIS: Sure am, son. Nevil's not here at the moment. He went pig shooting with his Uncle Booty.
TREVOR: Just my luck. I really wanted to see him.
MAVIS: Why?
TREVOR: Just to say hello.
MAVIS: Tell me, son, how do you know my Nevil?

TREVOR: Met him when I came out this way last year. [*Writing a note*] Can I leave this for him?

    MAVIS *looks down at his feet. She points to his sandals.*

MAVIS: How come you're wearin' women's sandals?
TREVOR: What? Oh, my sandals. They're men's sandals.
MAVIS: Sure. Sure they are. You just keep telling yourself that, son.
TREVOR: Ah, Mrs Dooley, is there a problem here?
MAVIS: Gotta girlfriend?
TREVOR: Say what?
MAVIS: A woman. Ya gotta woman? So, you like Jean Rhys, eh?
TREVOR: What are you trying to get at?
MAVIS: You city boys have funny ways, don'tcha? Queer ways.

    TREVOR *backs away from the door.*

TREVOR: Excuse me? Ah, Mrs Dooley, I don't know what you mean.

    MAVIS *moves scarily close to him.*

MAVIS: Enough is enough. Do ya love my Nevil?
TREVOR: What?! Oh, um, sure. He's a good friend of mine.
MAVIS: He's already gotta girlfriend and her name's Gracie.
TREVOR: Ah, yes, I see, Mrs Dooley.
MAVIS: [*to the audience*] It's clear to me now that Trevor and Nevil are you know what. That's why Nev's been gettin' doodee-dahed up, calling himself Jean. Mavis Dooley ain't nobody's fool.

    BOOTY *and* NEVIL *enter.* NEVIL *spots* TREVOR. *He rushes up to him.*

NEVIL: Trev!
TREVOR: Nev!
NEVIL: I can't believe you came all the way to Mandamooka just for me!

    He pulls TREVOR *aside.*

Listen, don't say a word to Mum about this, right? Jean Rhys, anything. She'll ruin it all.
TREVOR: Oh, well, okay. But are you sure?

    NEVIL *nods.*

BOOTY: What's going on here? [*To* TREVOR] Who're you, mate?
NEVIL: Trevor, meet my Uncle Booty.

BOOTY: You're not from around here, huh?
TREVOR: From Brisbane.
BOOTY: One of 'em flash city nancies, eh.

> BOOTY *looks* TREVOR *up and down, obviously not liking what he sees.*

NEVIL: Welcome to Mandamooka, Trevor.

> *They move into the kitchen where* MAVIS *sits at the table.*

Mum, can Trevor camp here for a few days?
MAVIS: Why?
NEVIL: He's my friend. Shit, I don't have to tell you everything.
MAVIS: He can camp in the spare room, right. Spare room, Nevil, you hear me!

> NEVIL *and* TREVOR *exit.* BOOTY *sits at the table with* MAVIS.

BOOTY: What's that bloke doing here?
MAVIS: Don't know. See the women's sandals he's wearing?
BOOTY: Be fucked!
MAVIS: Booty, I been thinkin' real hard 'bout Nevil. I'm starting to wonder if he was meant to be a girl. Like he's little bit man but mostly woman.
BOOTY: The boy's got balls, for crying out loud!
MAVIS: I dunno what's to become of him. Woman's had a gutful lyin' to everyone. Saying he's Jean. Where'd that sicko idea come from?
BOOTY: Got me stumped. Even the shootin' trip failed. Boy showed, pigs ran the other way.
MAVIS: We're fast runnin' outta time here. Me bones tell me that Jerry Reedman'll take his place. We just have to do something!
BOOTY: Only thing left to do now, teach him how to be a proper bloke. The hard way if need be.

> BOOTY *and* MAVIS *exit.*
>
> *Later. The kitchen.*
>
> *A boxing ring is set up. Four double-barrel drums sit opposite each other, connected by pieces of thick rope. A potato sack hangs from the ceiling.*
>
> TREVOR *sits on a double-barrel drum, watching* NEVIL *throw punches at the sack.* MAVIS *sits on another drum nearby.*

MAVIS: Be careful, Nevil. Don't hurt ya hands. You need to be fit for those selectors.

> NEVIL *hits the sack even harder.*

BOOTY: [*to* NEVIL] This'll knock the girl outta ya!

> BOOTY *starts shadowboxing.*

TREVOR: [*to* MAVIS] Guess this is the way of life in the bush for young men. Passage of manhood.

MAVIS: I wouldn't go that far.

> BOOTY *stands before* TREVOR.

BOOTY: On your feet, son!

TREVOR: Say what?

BOOTY: Come on, don't be a girl.

> BOOTY *tries to pull* TREVOR *to his feet.* TREVOR *holds the edge of the drum tightly.*

TREVOR: I can't fight. Wouldn't have a clue.

BOOTY: Talk shit. Off with that poxy shirt!

MAVIS: Booty, you leave him alone. Crackin' heads won't solve a bloody thing!

BOOTY: How the hell are they ever gonna be real men, eh? 'Specially him. [*Pointing to* NEVIL] Better he knows how to fight. Might save his own arse one of these days.

> BOOTY *manages to get* TREVOR *to his feet. He tries to drag him into the ring.*

TREVOR: No way. I can't box! Honestly, mate.

> BOOTY *grabs* TREVOR *in a fierce headlock.*

BOOTY: Don't be a big sheila. Come on, show me what you're made of!

> *Each time* TREVOR *tries to break free,* BOOTY *grips even harder.*

TREVOR: Ouch! Shit! Let me go.

NEVIL: For Christ's sake, leave him alone, Uncle!

MAVIS: Enough, Booty. Call it a day.

> *Finally,* BOOTY *gets* TREVOR *into the ring. He dances around him.* TREVOR *just stands there, unsure what to do. Tauntingly,* BOOTY *clips him under the ear.*

BOOTY: Don't be a sook. And don't stand there lookin' like an idiot. Fight!

> TREVOR *looks at* NEVIL *and* MAVIS: *what can I do?*

MAVIS: Break it up. Enough already, Booty.

BOOTY: This is no place for you, Mavis. Gone, get outta here!

> BOOTY *turns back to the ring.* TREVOR *throws a wild punch and accidentally hits him in the head.* BOOTY *crashes to the floor and lies there stunned. Dazed, he gets to his feet.*

NEVIL: Mum, you'd better do something. Quick! [*To* BOOTY] He didn't mean to!

> MAVIS *places herself defensively in front of* TREVOR.

TREVOR: It was an accident. A freak accident.

> BOOTY *grabs* TREVOR *by the shirt.*

BOOTY: Thought you couldn't fight? You've gotta bloody punch and a half on ya! When I think about it… way you look… no one would ever guess…

TREVOR: Guess what?

> BOOTY *gives* MAVIS *a quick glance.*

BOOTY: Talk to you later, man to man. Right?

MAVIS: No more of your stupid ideas, Booty. Enough is enough is enough!

> MAVIS *exits.*

♦ ♦ ♦ ♦ ♦

SCENE FIVE

MAVIS *and* GWEN *sit at the table with a bottle of Coke and a plate of lamingtons.*

MAVIS: What's this you wanna show me, Gwenny?

> GWEN *pulls out a wad of fifty-dollar notes from her handbag.*

GWEN: Darryl gave me this.

MAVIS: Bastard probably flogged it from his wife.

GWEN: Give us a break. He got that bungoo from a deal he made. Sold that old Jersey cow of his.

MAVIS: You shouldn't take the lying no-good-for-nothing back. All the trouble he's caused!
GWEN: Another funny thing is this. [*She pulls out a bag of white powder from her handbag.*] What'd ya make of that? Is he sending me a message?
MAVIS: Flour? He gave you a bag of flour? That bastard's some hide! Talk about ungrateful. What, your cookin' not good enough for him?

GWEN *throws the bag of powder on the table, angrily.*

GWEN: I dunno what Darryl's comin' at. What an arsehole thing to do to me!

MRS WARBY *enters.*

MRS WARBY: Yoo-hoo, Mavis! Just baked some lamingtons for morning tea.

MRS WARBY *pulls out a tray of lamingtons from her bag.*

MAVIS: Thanks, Mrs Warby, that's real nice of ya.
GWEN: Gotta go. Avon calling.

GWEN *exits.*

MAVIS: Woman's real busy today, Mrs Warby.

MRS WARBY *spots the bag of powder, grabs it and holds it up.*

MRS WARBY: Say, Mavis, what are you doing with this?
MAVIS: That's Gwen's. Plain flour, I think. Her idiot boyfriend gave it to her.
MRS WARBY: Don't mind if I borrow a cup? I need to bake another batch of lamingtons for the church fete.
MAVIS: Go ahead, Mrs Warby. Take the whole bag.
MRS WARBY: Thanks, Mavis. Very generous of you.

MRS WARBY *places the powder in her bag, then exits.*

SCENE SIX

MAVIS *sweeps the kitchen floor.*

MAVIS: [*to herself*] How'd this new lino get so bloody dirty?

NEVIL *enters, frocked, made-up.*

NEVIL: Mum, can I talk to you for a minute?
MAVIS: What about?
NEVIL: I know you won't like this… but I'm thinking of going to Brisbane. Gonna break away from football for a while.

> MAVIS *starts sweeping with jerky, angry movements.*

MAVIS: Break away from football. What sorta womba talk is that?! No, I don't wanna know. Talk to me when ya outta that dress and make sense.
NEVIL: It's my life. You can't force me to play football. Stop pushing me around, Mum.

> MAVIS *whacks the broom hard against the floor.*

MAVIS: How hard is it for you to go over to the clubhouse and throw the ball around?
NEVIL: I'll go over to the clubhouse when I'm ready!

> MAVIS *throws down the broom. She grabs a chair and sits, looking defeated.*

MAVIS: I've had it! Look, Nevil, I done walked me dirt track, the hard way. When I was your age I was on me hands and knees workin' for whitefellas. And you've the chance I've never had to do somethin' good with ya life. Football is the only way to do that. Don't throw it away by actin' stupid. Sometimes you just don't listen…

> NEVIL *gives her a hug.*

NEVIL: I love ya, Ma. I know this is hard—Oh, I don't even know—Maybe I don't understand—maybe we don't understand each other, I—Trevor understands me—
MAVIS: Oh, so this is what it's really all about, then. Trevor and his fancy ideas. You've changed, Nevil. You're not the same boy.
NEVIL: Face it, Mum, I've grown up. I need time to think more about my future. Just have faith in me.
MAVIS: Keep this up and you'll go down the same way as Uncle Booty. You'll have no future!
NEVIL: Football, football. Ever since I was a kid, that's all I ever heard round here. [*Rushing to exit, over his shoulder*] I hate football!
MAVIS: Now, that's a barefaced lie!

> NEVIL *exits.* DARRYL *enters. He watches* MAVIS *for a minute, then searches her kitchen, eyes roaming here, there.*

DARRYL: Where is it? Why'd I—? That stupid fucken Gwen! Aarrgghh!

He doesn't see what he's looking for and when MAVIS *looks up, he backtracks fast.* DARRYL *exits.* MAX *enters.*

MAX: How you been keeping, Mavis? Love, I'm here today on official business.

MAVIS: What's going on, Max?

MAX: I've received a missing-person complaint.

MAVIS: What?! Who's missing?

MAX *fumbles in his shirt pocket, pulls out a piece of paper, holds it up, squinting.*

MAX: Where are we here? Oh, here we are! Nevil? Nevil Dooley? Young Gracie claims he disappeared.

MAVIS: That silly girl. Got her wires crossed as usual. Max, Nevil's here.

MAX: He is? Well, next time you see that bloody Gracie, tell her to stop wasting my time. I've got better things to do.

MAVIS: I hear ya, Max.

MAX *goes to exit. He stops and turns around.*

MAX: Oh, and Mavis, love, got a call from Lyle Gould, narcs fella from Brisbane, about a drug dealer who's supposed to be in the area. Isaac Edge. Keep a close eye on things. Let me know of anything queer.

MAVIS: [*mouthing*] Queer?

MAX *exits.* DOROTHY *enters.*

DOROTHY: [*waving to* MAX] Max, over here! I've found your man!

MAVIS: [*to the audience*] I've a gut premonition that all me lies are gonna catch up soon. Nevil will be found out and his footy career will be cactus. I curse the day that boy found me frocks!

◆ ◆ ◆ ◆ ◆

SCENE SEVEN

MAVIS *is making breakfast, piling Tim Tams and lamingtons into a cereal bowl, topping it off with a good splash of milk.* TREVOR *enters.*

MAVIS: Mornin'.
TREVOR: Morning.

MAVIS: Sit down.

> *He sits at the table.* MAVIS *hands him the bowl and a glass of Coke.*

Here, I made this special, like. Might even put hairs on ya chest, eh.

> TREVOR *looks at the plate, perplexed.*

TREVOR: Breakfast?

MAVIS: Bingo.

TREVOR: I, well, Mrs Dooley…

MAVIS: No need to be tongue-tied, son. I like to see that ya grateful. Matter of fact, woman's famous for her cookin' round these parts.

> TREVOR *eats a lamington.*

TREVOR: Very nice, Mrs Dooley.

MAVIS: Listen here, Trevor, Nevil used to be normal once. Now he's all outta shape. I'm wondering why.

TREVOR: Ah, how to explain this? Mrs Dooley, Nevil's artistic vision is cramped in this town. And I'm here to help him release his creative ideas.

MAVIS: Creative ideas, my foot. But, listen, there's a way you can help and that's by helping me get Nevil over to the selectors. Football is his future.

TREVOR: I understand, Mrs Dooley. [*To himself*] Really, what can I say here? Nevil just needs a little space to explore his literary capabilities.

> MAVIS *contemplates him for a second. She laughs.*

MAVIS: Biggest loada crock I done ever heard! [*To the audience*] Nevil seems to have gotten worse with him around. He's effluencing Nevil. [*Pointing to her head*] Big ache here, tellin' me Nevil's on the fast track to nowhere. Woman'll just have to try harder.

> TREVOR *makes his way to exit.* GRACIE *enters, stoned, joint in hand. She rushes at* MAVIS *and grabs her in a tight hug.*

GRACIE: I love you, Mum.

MAVIS: I love you too, Gracie. But pull yourself together, girl. I've got a visitor.

> GRACIE *pushes the joint at* TREVOR.

GRACIE: Wanna toke?

TREVOR: You're Gracie?
GRACIE: What of it?

   MAVIS *steers* TREVOR *out the door.*

MAVIS: [*in a low voice*] Go on now, Trevor. Be gone. Hurry.

   TREVOR *exits.*

GRACIE: Who's that bloke?
MAVIS: That's… oh, Nevil's football buddy. From Brisbane.
GRACIE: What's up with those sandals?
MAVIS: Gracie, why the hell have you been spreadin' talk that Nevil's missing?
GRACIE: Because he is, isn't he?
MAVIS: The bloody shame! Had Max here and everything. But Nevil's home now. And, love, he hasn't been himself lately.
GRACIE: Why doesn't he want to see me all of a sudden? Sounds real suss.
MAVIS: Nothin' suss here, Gracie. Nevil's just real busy now. Polishin' his footy boots. Come back later and see him.

   GRACIE *spots a pair of brilliant red g-strings on the floor. She picks them up and waves them before* MAVIS.

GRACIE: Who the fuck owns these?
MAVIS: Oh, that's just… um, just an old dishrag, Gracie.

   MAVIS *snatches them, hiding them behind her back.*

I use them to keep me pots clean. Special fibre in 'em, see.
GRACIE: What?
MAVIS: Special fibre. Keeps the pots clean.
GRACIE: That's a lie! Nevil's got another girl! Fucken knew it! That arsehole's in his room! Too gutless to face me. To tell me our engagement's off! To think of all that love stuff he told me… the ring… that special night. How could he?

   GRACIE *exits.*

MAVIS: [*to the audience*] Ya gotta love the girl but she's, well, you know, gets a bit up here. [*Pointing to her head*] All that happy weed. No tellin' what she might come at.

◆◆◆◆◆

SCENE EIGHT

NEVIL, MAVIS *and* TREVOR *sit at the table.*

MAVIS: [*to* NEVIL] Me blood pressure's playin' up again. If ya don't get over to the clubhouse soon, I'll end up in hospital. Blood pressure will kill me. That's a fact.

NEVIL: Don't play sorry Doris with me, Mum. It won't work.

TREVOR *raises his hand.*

TREVOR: Mrs Dooley, Mrs Dooley, can I say something here? Thing is, Nevil wants to explore other opportunities in his life.

MAVIS: Other opportunities, my black foot. Trevor, shut ya cakehole!

NEVIL: [*to* TREVOR] Like I told you. Never hears me.

MAVIS: [*to* NEVIL] What you really need to do is to get that shit sorted out in ya head. Have a yarn to Dr Chin.

NEVIL: You think I've got head problems now?!

MAVIS: [*to* TREVOR] Worst thing in the world to tell a madman he's mad. It's like asking an alkie if he's a drunk.

NEVIL: Jesus, get off my back. Okay, okay, you win this one. I'll go see the selectors. Just this once!

MAVIS: That's all a woman wanted to hear. Tidy yaself up before you leave the house. Footy mates see you gussied-up like that, it'll be the last frock you'll ever wear.

NEVIL *exits. Pig dogs bark.*

BOOTY: [*offstage*] Down, bastards. Man's got no fucken pig meat today.

BOOTY *enters. He walks up behind* TREVOR *who turns around.*

Oh, it's you. Good thing you're here. Listen, you wanna make some bungoo?

TREVOR: What?

BOOTY: Got a boxing ring set up in the backyard. You'll be knucklin' Mad Dog. Crazy bastard. But you can take him out, with that deadly right hook.

TREVOR: What right hook? [*Dawning on him*] Oh, no! Booty, I don't want any part of it!

BOOTY: Gonna be bare knuckles. No pussy ever fought bare knuckles, eh. Five hundred bucks is on ya. Now, this is what ya gotta watch

with him. [*He starts shadowboxing.*] He lands one on ya, you'll be pissin' blood for a week!
TREVOR: Jesus! But, but I can't fight!
BOOTY: Too late, you're already in. Get ya arse out to the yard, otherwise the knuckling starts here in the kitchen.
TREVOR: No. No, I don't see… No, I can't. I have to say no on this one.
MAVIS: Wake up to yourself, Booty! Trevor's not like those other rough bastards.
BOOTY: Nev'll be fighting too.
MAVIS: Hey, hang on. Knuckling won't solve anything, Booty.
BOOTY: That little white boy can rumble. I can make some bungoo from him. Buy ya new curtains. There you go, Mave.
MAVIS: You leave the boys alone. We've enough trouble here already.
BOOTY: You just be there, sonny.

    BOOTY *exits.*

TREVOR: [*to himself*] What have I got myself involved with here? There's no way I can do that. I'm not a violent man.
MAVIS: [*to the audience*] A boxing match won't make Nevil normal again. He'll get hurt. Those selectors don't wanna busted-up player on the team. Woman'll have to make sure the boy stays safe. But, Jesus, where will all this end?

    Later. The kitchen.

    The boxing ring is set up. Plastic buckets and grubby old towels sit at opposite corners of the ring. Scattered randomly are a few double-barrel drums.

    MAVIS *and* GWEN *and* MRS WARBY *crouch down behind the drums.* TREVOR *is perched on a drum, near the ring.* NEVIL *is over in the corner, biting his nails.*

    BOOTY *enters, notepad in hand. He checks the ring, measuring it with his feet, adjusts the ropes, then checks the towels and buckets.*

Gwen, we've gotta stop this! Nevil can't fight. He doesn't know how to. What's a woman to do?
GWEN: Hang on. Let me think. Shit, things are happening too fast. Think, Gwendoline, think!

MAD DOG *enters. He shadowboxes his way into the room, looking around for his opponent.*

MAD DOG: Who's the cunt who wants a piece a this?!

He hits himself hard in the chest. NEVIL *shrinks back against a drum.*

GWEN: Mavis, look there!

MAVIS: Who's that?!

GWEN: Mad Dog, real bad arse. Geez, Booty wouldn't let a dirty bastard like him fight Nevil. Surely not.

MAVIS: This has to be stopped before Nevil gets killed, hurt, murdered.

BOOTY: [*to* MAD DOG *and* NEVIL] Righto, boys, the rules of this match are—there are none. Let's rumble.

NEVIL *backs away.*

NEVIL: Hang on! Uncle, you didn't tell me that I had to fight! You said it was just a—You lied! No, leave me out of this!

BOOTY *shoves* NEVIL *towards the ring.*

BOOTY: In the ring, Nevil. Now!

NEVIL *backs away from him.*

NEVIL: No!

MAD DOG: [*to* NEVIL] 'Boo-hoo, where's me mummy?' Come on, crybaby bitch, take a crack at a real man!

MAD DOG *points to* NEVIL*'s shorts where a pair of frilly knickers peek over the waistband.*

And what the fuck is that?! Lookee here, I got meself a faggot!

NEVIL *charges at* MAD DOG. MAD DOG *lands him a bone-crunching right hook to the side of the head.* NEVIL *hits the deck hard, rolling around, holding his head.*

NEVIL: Shit! Oh, Jesus!

TREVOR *slips out his mobile phone and calls the cops.* MRS WARBY *scurries over to* BOOTY *and taps him on the shoulder.*

MRS WARBY: Booty, stop this right now! The Lord doesn't approve of this behaviour. Let Nevil go!

BOOTY: Mrs Warby, what in the blue hell are you doing here? Go home.

MRS WARBY *pretends to leave but crouches down behind a drum, watching the ring closely.* MAD DOG *kicks* NEVIL *hard in the ribcage.*

MAD DOG: Up, pussy boy!

   MAVIS *pelts towards the ring.*

MAVIS: You bastard! Leave my son alone!

   BOOTY *pushes her back.*

BOOTY: Thought I told you sheilas to stay away. No women allowed!

MAVIS: You've just gone too far, Booty. End this now!

   GWEN *rushes out from behind the drum.*

GWEN: [*to* MAD DOG] Pick on someone ya own size, you big ugly galoot!

MRS WARBY: Oh Lord, Ivy Warby asks you to save this poor boy!

   Shakily, NEVIL *gets to his feet. He throws a punch but misses.* MAD DOG *slams him back to the ground.*

BOOTY: Stop fucking round, Nevil. You can do better than that.

   BOOTY *circles the ring, throwing his fists.*

GWEN: Run away, Nevil!

MAVIS: [*to* BOOTY] He's gonna kill Nevil. [*To* NEVIL] Lay down your fists, son. Don't fight him. Be a better man, walk away!

   NEVIL *stumbles out of the ring, favouring his ribcage.*

MAD DOG: [*to* NEVIL] Hey, Dooley! I fucked ya mother. Fucked that old goer real good. [*Thrusting his hips*] And she loved it, man!

TREVOR: Oh, my God!

   NEVIL *glances at his mother. She looks horrified, angry. Enraged, he gets back into the ring, more confident and agile. He shapes up.* MAD DOG *laughs.*

NEVIL: No one talks about my mother that way. You shithead!

   NEVIL *lets rip with a jaw-shattering right hook, putting* MAD DOG *on his arse. He goes across to his mother and puts a protective arm around her.*

Come on, let's go inside, Mum.

   MAD DOG *gets up, dazed.*

MRS WARBY: [*to* MAD DOG] Keep your paws to yourself, Mr Big Shot! You've no right to beat on Nevil. If I was your mother I'd wash out your potty mouth with soap.

> MRS WARBY *slams him hard in the gut with her bag.*

MAD DOG: The fuck're you on about?

MRS WARBY: Why, you… you animal!

> MRS WARBY *lets rip again, hitting him even harder.*

MAD DOG: Owwhh, you fucking old cow!

> MAD DOG *gasps, doubling over.* BOOTY *goes across to* TREVOR.

BOOTY: Your turn.

TREVOR: Not on your life!

> *Police sirens. Flashing red and blue lights.*

MAVIS: The gungies. Nevil, come on. Hurry!

> MAD DOG *exits.* MAVIS, MRS WARBY, NEVIL *and* GWEN *hide behind the drums.* BOOTY *hooks over to the other drum and crouches down.* TREVOR *stands frozen, not sure what to do.*
>
> *Pig dogs start an uproar, growling, barking.*

MAX: [*offstage*] Holy shit! Down, boy. Nice dog.

> MAX *and* LYLE *enter.*

LYLE: [*looking around*] Dodgy bastard's done a runner.

MAX: Oh… he has?

> LYLE *spots* BOOTY*'s thongs poking out from behind the drum. He goes over to the drum and hits it hard.*

LYLE: Playtime's over, Mary. Toys away. On your feet, Doiley!

> BOOTY *jumps up.*

BOOTY: Piss off. I haven't done anything wrong.

LYLE: So you'd have me believe.

> LYLE *grabs* BOOTY, *leading him towards the exit. On his way out, he spots* TREVOR. *He quickly shoves* BOOTY *at* MAX. *He spins on* TREVOR, *grabbing him roughly.*

My, my, my. Look who we have here. Mr Isaac Edge. Not such a smart bastard after all, eh.

TREVOR: Who? Hey, hold on! I'm the one who rang!
LYLE: Thought you could outfox the fox, huh? Come along, pretty boy Floyd. Your arse is all mine.

> LYLE *forces* TREVOR *out the exit.* MAX *and* BOOTY *follow.*

MAVIS: [*to the audience*] Well, that was a right cock-up. So much for Booty's plan of making Nevil a man. Fact is, Nevil will never be like his uncle. And with the snorters on the job now, things can only get worse. Woman's really at the end of her tether.

> MAVIS, MRS WARBY *and* GWEN *exit.*

END OF ACT ONE

ACT TWO

SCENE ONE

The Mandamooka cop shop. There's a couple of chairs in the corner, a typewriter on the table and a few tattered notices on a cork board.

MAX *stands at the table trying to organise a sheaf of papers.* MAVIS *enters.*

MAVIS: Max, what's going on? Where's Booty and Trevor?

Flustered, MAX *drops the papers. He bends down and picks them up.*

MAX: Mavis, I'm sorry about all this. Booty's down in the cell, cooling off. I'll release him shortly. As for that other fella, well, he isn't Trevor Davidson. His real name is Isaac Edge. Biggest dope dealer this side of the dingo fence.

MAVIS: You've gotta be joking! How do you know he's Isaac Edge?

MAX: Detective Gould from the Brisbane narcotics squad has identified our man.

MAVIS: I just don't believe it.

MAX: Love, between me and you, stay clear of this one. Gould's out to burn someone. Those old narc boys are a tough bunch.

MAVIS: But can you prove Trevor's been sellin' drugs?

MAX: We have witnesses, that's all I can say.

MAVIS: Can I see him?

MAX: Come along then.

> MAX *leads* MAVIS *to the cells.* TREVOR, *sitting cross-legged on the floor, is biting his fingernails, looking petrified. On seeing* MAVIS, *he jumps up.*

TREVOR: Mrs Dooley, thank God you're here!

MAX: Watch yourself, fella. [*To* MAVIS] Be outside if you need me.

MAVIS: [*to* TREVOR] Love, what's going on?

TREVOR: I've given them my business card and told them to phone Brisbane.

MAVIS: I reckon they've mixed you up with someone else, son.

TREVOR: It seems… that's it! Your neighbour and another woman were in here talking to the cop. The big-hair woman said something about me having drugs in my briefcase, then something else about Jean Rhys, drugs, the selectors…

MAVIS: Selectors?! Now why would she…? Yeah, that'd be Dotty bloody Reedman. But why mention the selectors? What the—?

TREVOR: It's all been some terrible mistake! All I've done is to come here to help Nevil.

MAVIS: Actually, Trevor, you haven't helped Nevil at all. In fact, since you turned up, he's worse. But I know what it's all about—you want Nev to go to the city to be one of them transvestays!

TREVOR: A transvestite. Nevil's not like—I mean, he's—

MAVIS: Fulla happy weed?

TREVOR: How'd you come up with that?!

MAVIS: Never you mind. You'd just better pull ya head in quick smart! That D's here to haul you off to the slammer.

TREVOR: I haven't done anything. Nevil knows what's going on. Ask him.

MAVIS: Keep Nevil outta this. Boy's got enough head trouble already.

TREVOR: Oh, shit! What can I do? Mrs Dooley, listen, listen hard—Can you get me a lawyer?

MAVIS: Only lawyer-type round these parts is old Shirl from Legal Aid. She won't help. Not today. There's a big jackpot on at bingo. Fifty bucks.

TREVOR: Why me?!

MAVIS: No use bein' a bawl-baby. Won't do ya much good, son. Look, I know you're not one of those druggie fellas and the only thing—

MAX and LYLE enter.

MAX: [*to* MAVIS] Step outside for a minute, love. The detective needs to have a little talk to our friend here.

LYLE: [*to* TREVOR] On your feet, Sally.

MAVIS: For sure, that D's gonna sew the boy up.

MAVIS pretends to leave. She sidles up the wall, eavesdropping on LYLE and TREVOR. TREVOR is sitting in a chair, nervous, scared. LYLE circles him, menacingly.

LYLE: Had it set from the git-go, didn't you, Edge?!

TREVOR: I don't know what you're talking about. Phone Brisbane. I'm Trevor Davidson. Senior editor from Crossroads Publishing.

> MAVIS *moves a little closer to the wall, trying her best to listen in.* LYLE *stands before* TREVOR, *cracking his knuckles.*

LYLE: Editor, yeah, sure. Do I look like a cockhead to you?! You can't pull the Stetson over my eyes, cowboy. I know all about your identity scams. Fess up, girlfriend!

TREVOR: You can't hold me here. You've no right. I wanna lawyer!

LYLE: Smart cunt, eh!

> LYLE *punches* TREVOR *in the gut.* TREVOR *screams, doubling over in agony.*

TREVOR: Oh, my God! Leave me alone!

MAVIS: Oh, Christ, what's a woman to do?

LYLE: I've got you pegged, Edge. Know all about the skag you've been trying to sell. Spill your guts!

TREVOR: There's nothing to say. I'm here for business.

LYLE: I know all about your 'business'. You and this Jean Rhys.

TREVOR: What?! You know about Jean Rhys?

LYLE: You admit it? Where is she?

TREVOR: I… I, um, can't tell you. It's just that I can't say…

LYLE: I'll get it out of you.

TREVOR: Ask Mrs Dooley. She knows the truth!

LYLE: Using those pretty-boy looks on that old Doiley sheila, eh? What, she's involved too?

TREVOR: No! Oh God, no! Right, I've had enough. I'm leaving. This is illegal.

> TREVOR *tentatively stands.* LYLE *shoves him back down into the chair.*

LYLE: Down, Jane. I'm not done yet.

TREVOR: I'm suing you for assault.

LYLE: Sue this, you cunt!

> LYLE *grabs* TREVOR *and starts pushing, shoving, prodding, punching him around.* TREVOR *fights to get away. He falls off the chair, grabs* LYLE's *ankle and bites down hard.* TREVOR *makes for the exit and runs headfirst into* MAVIS.

MAVIS: The bloody hell's goin' on here?

LYLE: Bastard! Stinking bastard!

> TREVOR *hides behind* MAVIS.

MAVIS: Gould, you leave this kid alone. If he's Edge then I'm a white woman.

> MAX *enters.*

MAX: Ah, Lyle, he's not Isaac Edge. Wrong man. Mistaken identity, mate.

MAVIS: Gould, you keep ya hands to yourself.

LYLE: [*to* TREVOR] Sorry about that, mate.

> LYLE *exits.* MAX *motions* TREVOR *and* MAVIS *over to his desk.*

MAX: I'm sorry, Mr Davidson. We had to check you out.

MAVIS: Woman can't understand ya, Max. Thinking Trevor's a drug dealer. Clock the boy's sandals.

MAX: Good point, Mavis.

> MAX *resumes shuffling papers.*

TREVOR: [*to* MAVIS] That bastard detective assaulted me. I should sue him and this shitty little cop shop, too.

MAVIS: Never mind, love. You're lucky ya not a blackfella, otherwise you'd have been crawling outta there. [*To the audience*] Funny, how things only went haywire since Nevil started to be a woman and Trevor turned up on me doorstep. Has this something to do with them? Have they both been lying to me? It's like some nightmare a woman can't get out of! And who the bleedin' hell is Isaac Edge?!

> TREVOR *and* MAVIS *exit.*

SCENE TWO

MAVIS *and a frocked* NEVIL *are sitting at the table.* GRACIE *is standing at the other end, looking seriously pissed off. She grabs a cup, smashes it to the floor, then picks up a plate and hurls it furiously at the wall. From her back jeans pocket, she grabs a handful of Mars Bars and starts launching them at* NEVIL.

GRACIE: What the fuck do you mean, 'feminine side'?

NEVIL *dodges the Mars Bars, ducking beneath the table.*

NEVIL: Shit! Stop it!

MAVIS *jumps up, pulls out a chair.*

MAVIS: Gracie, settle down. Here, have a seat, love.

Out of Mars Bars, GRACIE *plonks onto the chair.* NEVIL *gets back onto his chair.*

NEVIL: It's, um, sort of like men have a feminine side. That we have portions of Adam and Eve inside of us and—

GRACIE: Oh. Well, that'd mean I gotta man inside of me, then? That really I'm half man?

NEVIL: Something along those lines. It's a subconscious process that has to be developed. Encouraged to come out.

GRACIE: Like when you're a poofter and tell the world?

MAVIS: Gracie, don't use that word! Say gay, Gracie, gay.

GRACIE: And why the fuck would ya wanna call yourself Jean Rhys?

MAVIS: Gracie, Jean Rhys don't exist. She's all in Nevil's 'magination. It's bulldust, girl.

GRACIE: Whatcha talkin' about?

NEVIL: Jean Rhys was a writer. She wrote about a woman going mad. Antoinette Cosway, married Mr Rochester then he took her to England. She became the woman in the attic. Bertha Rochester in *Jane Eyre*.

MAVIS & GRACIE: [*together*] Shut ya cakehole, Nevil!

NEVIL: I'm sorry, Gracie. It's just that I wanna do other things with my life. As I told you before, follow your dreams.

GRACIE: You lost the plot or what?! Are you fellas mad? What are youse on?

NEVIL: Gracie, just hear me out.

GRACIE: Nevil, I've had your shit! I'm not gonna sit around, waiting for you. Girl'd be a deadset idiot. The engagement's off!

GRACIE *makes her way to the exit.* MAVIS *bolts after her.*

MAVIS: Gracie girl, stop! It was all just a joke. One big joke. Ha, ha! See, I'm laughin'.

GRACIE *exits.*

◆ ◆ ◆ ◆ ◆

SCENE THREE

MAVIS *is washing up some pots and pans.* NEVIL *is at the table reading a book, frocked and made-up.* DOROTHY *enters.*

DOROTHY: Busy day, Dooley?
MAVIS: Shove off, Reedman.
DOROTHY: Coppers got your friend, eh?
MAVIS: What?
DOROTHY: Your friend. The druggie dealer.
MAVIS: For cryin' out loud, Reedman, give it a rest. Stop cartin' yarns. It's causing nothin' but strife.
DOROTHY: I saw what I saw.
MAVIS: What you saw and thought you saw are two different things!
DOROTHY: Looks like he's pulled a swifty on you, Dooley.

    NEVIL *stands up to reveal his dress.* DOROTHY *spots him.*

Nevil's really fucked up this time! Frocks and drugs don't go down too well with the selectors. It's all Jerry's now. Score again for the Reedmans!
MAVIS: Dorothy, what I have ever done to you, woman?
DOROTHY: Let's just say I've never liked you, Dooley.
MAVIS: Reedman, just stop and take a good look at yaself. Ya have it in you to be a better person, you know.
DOROTHY: Piss off!

    GWEN *enters, panicked.*

GWEN: [*to* MAVIS] Where's the flour? Where's Darryl's flour?
DOROTHY: Oh, and Gwen, think that you're the only one with dibs on Darryl? Guess what, that's where ya wrong!
GWEN: Darryl wouldn't touch you if you were the last woman in Mandamooka!

    DOROTHY *exits.*

MAVIS: Just goes to show what an idiot he is. Womba.
GWEN: That flour, Mave. He wants it back. Where is it? Who'd a thought he'd get so worked up over a bag of flour.
MAVIS: [*to the audience*] There's something not quite right here. When I think about it—Darryl, Dottie, Trevor, the drug dealer, Jean Rhys, Isaac Edge—Somehow it all seems—Hey, I've worked it out!

◆ ◆ ◆ ◆ ◆

SCENE FOUR

Later. NEVIL, MAVIS, GWEN, MRS WARBY *and* TREVOR *are at the table, drinking tea.* MRS WARBY *takes out a tray of lamingtons from her handbag and places them on the table.*

MRS WARBY: Saved some of this batch from the church fete. Anyone want one?

> *Everyone looks sick and shakes their heads.* MRS WARBY *starts eating them.*

MAVIS: Mrs Warby. But now what—?

MRS WARBY: Mavis, I'm sorry. I've been a very foolish woman. Dorothy had me convinced that you, Nevil, Trevor and some woman called Jean Rhys were involved with selling drugs.

MAVIS: Mrs Warby, think hard now, did she mention Isaac Edge?

MRS WARBY: Isaac Edge? Oh yes, she did. Said that Trevor is a dead ringer for Isaac. Make of that what you will.

MAVIS: Somewhere, somehow, someone got the wrong message. Isaac Edge has to be Darryl Kane.

GWEN: That's it! Darryl said he was gonna get you and Nevil back. Whatever that means. Right, that bastard's got some talkin' to do.

MAVIS: Gwen, no, stop. Don't worry about it.

> GWEN *exits.*

NEVIL: [*to everyone*] How'd Jean Rhys get brought into this?

MAVIS: Seems she's everywhere but nowhere.

NEVIL: I didn't expect for things to turn out like this. Jean Rhys was an author and—

> *Pig dogs bark.* BOOTY *and* TREVOR *enter.*

TREVOR: Nevil! There's trouble! Jean Rhys trouble! The cops are after her. You've just got to tell everyone the truth.

BOOTY: What the fuck's going on now?

MAVIS: Darryl Kane set us up.

BOOTY: [*to* NEVIL *and* TREVOR] You fellas wanna settle a score? You gonna let the skinny white prick get away with this?

> TREVOR *shrinks back away.* NEVIL *shakes his head: no way.*

MAVIS: Booty, leave the boys alone. Don't want any more gungies here.

BOOTY: Right, you blokes, let's go teach Kane a lesson.
MAVIS: No, Booty! I'll handle this.
BOOTY: Mavis, ya couldn't knock dust off a damper.

> MRS WARBY *roots around in her bag. She pulls out a tray of lamingtons, a bible and lays them on the table. She rummages again, pulling out a shotgun.*

MRS WARBY: I'll deal with him.
BOOTY: Put that gun down, woman!

> MRS WARBY *slides a shell into the gun chamber.*

MRS WARBY: I'm afraid the Lord has spoken. It's my duty to bring this to an end. And, quite frankly, Ivy Warby has had enough!
MAVIS: [*to everyone, including the audience*] If she starts firing, take cover!
MRS WARBY: Mr Kane is now stuck up a river of poop without a paddle.

> MRS WARBY *looks through the scope.* NEVIL *moves tentatively towards her.*

NEVIL: Give me the gun.
MAVIS: Put that shottie down before ya kill somebody!

> MRS WARBY *fools around with the bullet chamber.*

MRS WARBY: Seems this thing's stuck.

> MRS WARBY *waves the gun around.* GRACIE *enters. At first she doesn't see* MRS WARBY. *She hears a click, turns and spots* MRS WARBY.

GRACIE: Holy shit!

> GRACIE *jumps back. The shotgun explodes. Everyone drops to the floor, some scramble to hide beneath the table, covering their ears.* MRS WARBY *inspects the gun.*

Jesus! That was a fucked thing to do, Mrs Warby.
TREVOR: Shut up. Everyone be quiet.

> *Police sirens. The flashing of red and blue lights.*

BOOTY: That's all we need, the fucken snorters again!

> LYLE *crouches down, loudspeaker in hand,* MAX *alongside.* LYLE *talks through the speaker.*

LYLE: Jean Rhys, Detective Lyle Gould here. Release the hostages!
ALL: What?

LYLE: Any demands? Speak to me.
MAVIS: [*to everyone*] Demands? What's that ratbag talkin' about?

> MAX *warily tries to take the loudspeaker from* LYLE.

MAX: Lyle, say Lyle, can you let me talk to Mavis?
LYLE: [*to* MAVIS] Jean Rhys, down your arms. Come out of the house!

> MAX *finally snatches the speaker.*

MAX: Testing, testing! Mavis, love, it's Max here. Is everyone all right?

> LYLE *goes for his mobile phone.*

MAVIS: What's this about? I haven't done anything.
GRACIE: [*to* MAVIS] Phone's ringing.
MAVIS: You get it, Gracie.

> GRACIE *picks up the phone, speaking low.*

MAX: Cooee! Cooee! Mavis, can you hear me? Love, do you want me to get Shirl from Legal Aid? Anyone hurt? I can get Dr Chin.
LYLE: [*into his phone*] Those are your demands? You want us to get you five Mars Bars, a slab of beer and a joint?
GRACIE: [*into the phone*] Drop it off on the front steps, eh.

> LYLE *snatches the loudspeaker back.* MAX *snatches it back again.* LYLE *snatches it back once more.* MAX *spots* MAVIS *and waves.* MAX *over the loudspeaker.*

MAX: Mavis… Mavis, love…
LYLE: [*to* MAX] What the fuck are you doing?! Sit there, shut up and call for backup!
MAX: Lyle, you've got it all wrong.
LYLE: You're hopeless. Pull yourself together, man. Those black bastards are gonna start throwing lead at us soon.
MAX: You've made this situation far worse.
LYLE: Mate, they're all the fucking same to me. Bastards will be in there, scoped-up, ready to blow our arses to kingdom come.
MAVIS: [*to everyone*] I'll have to go out there and set Max straight.
LYLE: Jean Rhys, come out or we'll be coming in!

> GRACIE *takes a couple of lamingtons from the table and eats them. Finished, she picks up the gun and jokingly aims it at* BOOTY.

BOOTY: Gracie, don't mess around with that! Put it down, girl!

> GRACIE, *stoned, laughs wildly, waving the gun around.*

GRACIE: Bang. Gotcha!

> LYLE *bolts across to the house, gun drawn. He spots* GRACIE. *He bends low, taking cover near the table.*

LYLE: Drop the gun, Jean Rhys! On the floor! Hands behind your head!

> GRACIE *looks around, wondering where the voice is coming from.*

GRACIE: Who's there?

> LYLE *charges at* GRACIE, *knocking her to the floor. He handcuffs her.*

MAX: No, Lyle, for God's sake! No!
GRACIE: Get off me, fucking snorter!

> LYLE *gets up, scanning the room. He spots* MAVIS *and charges at her.*

LYLE: Drop to the floor, Mrs Doiley! Move, move!
MAVIS: It's Dooley, not friggin' Doiley!
BOOTY: It was Mrs Warby.
NEVIL: I made up Jean Rhys!
MAVIS: The real Isaac Edge is Darryl Kane!
GRACIE: Freaky, man.

> *Blackout.*

◆◆◆◆◆

SCENE FIVE

The next day. MAVIS, MRS WARBY, TREVOR, BOOTY *and* NEVIL *are all seated around the table, waiting patiently.*

MAX *and* LYLE *enter.* LYLE *pushes a handcuffed* DARRYL KANE *into the room.*

LYLE: [*to everyone*] Finally caught our man, Darryl Kane, a.k.a. Isaac Edge.
MAX: Found him hanging around your place, Mavis.
LYLE: Looking for a certain bag of something.
DARRYL: [*to* LYLE] Fuck you! [*To* MAVIS] I know you flogged me gear, bitch hole.

BOOTY: What gear?

    DARRYL *lunges at* MAVIS.

MAX: The drugs, Booty. The drugs!

BOOTY: Drugs? What drugs?

DARRYL: How stupid could a man be, giving Gwen the fucken stash.

MAVIS: Sweet f-ing Jesus! The lamingtons. Mrs Warby. The fete. The church. Holy shit!

MAX: But, Kane, why give Gwenny the stash?

DARRYL: Didn't wanna get caught with that load. Not with you cockheads on the prowl. With Dorothy's big mouth it was easy to fuck them over.

    DARRYL *nods at* MAVIS *and* NEVIL.

MAVIS: That bloody Reedman.

NEVIL: [*to* DARRYL] Man, you need help.

MAVIS: [*to* DARRYL] Get Dr Chin to take a look at that crook head of yours, sonny boy. 'Cause you've got some wires hangin' loose in there.

BOOTY: Fucken ratbag!

    The phone rings. BOOTY *answers it.* GWEN *enters.*

GWEN: Darryl?

    DARRYL *struggles hard against* LYLE.

DARRYL: Gwenny! [*To* LYLE] Let me go, you prick! Come on, Gwenny, help a man out!

    LYLE *grabs hold of* DARRYL *and wallops him on the head.*

LYLE: Time to move on, sister. We've some talking to do.

    LYLE *leads* DARRYL *away.*

DARRYL: [*over his shoulder*] Love you, Gwenny.

GWEN: Don't love you, ya wanker.

    LYLE, DARRYL, MAX *and* GWEN *exit.* BOOTY *hangs up the phone.*

BOOTY: Just got news that Nevil's been picked by the selectors to be on the state team.

MAVIS: I knew it.

NEVIL: Mum, I'm sorry but, but Saturday's my last game.

MAVIS: Your last? What do ya mean?

NEVIL: Mum, I'm sorry for everything. Truly. Fact is, Trevor's an editor.

It's like this, I've been writing for a while now and Trevor's here to help get my book published.

MAVIS: What?! Writing? What do you mean, 'writing'? Oh, this is another joke, is it?

BOOTY: It better fucken not be.

NEVIL: Mum, I'm gonna put it to you straight. I'm a grown man now and wanna live my life the way I choose, not the way you want—

MAVIS: Since when have I ever told you what to do?

NEVIL: You, Uncle Booty, the town, everyone's had a say in my life.

MAVIS: What the bleedin' hell has the town to do with it?

NEVIL: Everything. Because of what happened to Booty.

MAVIS: But what was I supposed to do, Nevil? Stand back and let someone ruin your dreams.

NEVIL: I never cared what anyone else thought! Mum, they've always been your dreams, not mine. Admit it, you know it's true.

MAVIS: But all the grief... the drugs, cops, guns!

BOOTY: All this bullshit 'cause ya wanted to write a book?

NEVIL: I didn't count on all that other stuff going down. But I had to do things my way, take my chances. Break away from what everyone else thought. I'm just sorry that everything got out of hand.

MAVIS: Okay then, what's this book about?

NEVIL: It's about a Murri woman, Lucinda, living in the bush, trying to rebuild a life that's been destroyed by gossips and lies.

MAVIS: But why write as a woman?

NEVIL: It comes down to this, it's easier to be a man in this town than to be a woman. Because a woman's got to be as tough as a man and not show it.

BOOTY: Biggest loada shit man's ever heard.

TREVOR: [*raising his hand*] Mrs Dooley, Mrs Dooley, can I say something here? Nevil was ashamed of his own talent. Didn't think anyone in this town would understand him. I predict great things for Nevil. His novel is brilliantly achieved. And Lucinda is a unique, unforgettable character.

MAVIS: What can a woman say here? Except, Nevil, ya sure make your old mother real proud! You always come good in the end, eh.

> NEVIL *gets up, goes over and cuddles* MAVIS, *then* BOOTY. GRACIE *enters.*

GRACIE: Come to tell youse all that I'm blowin' this joint. Nevil, good

luck. Girl's got some serious life shit to do. A new job and all. Doing the Bullya Avon run with Gwen.
BOOTY: Gracie girl, keep ya nose clean, eh.
GRACIE: Count on it, Uncle.
MAVIS: Follow ya dreams, Gracie, 'cause in the end, that's all ya got. And, love, ain't no one in this world can tell you otherwise. [*To* NEVIL] Guess it's time for you to do things ya own way, Nevil. Go into the world and make yourself a man.

◆ ◆ ◆ ◆ ◆

SCENE SIX

The next day. Mandamooka football oval.

BOOTY, GWEN, MAX, MAVIS, MRS WARBY, DOROTHY *and* TREVOR *are waiting for the game to begin.*

The sound of a whistle. NEVIL *enters, charging past, football in hand.*

VOICE-OVER: Young Dooley has the ball. He's like lightning! That kid can go!

    MAVIS *spots* DOROTHY *and moves across to her.*

DOROTHY: Score for Mooka, Nevil!
MAVIS: [*to the audience*] Wonders will never cease! [*Watching* NEVIL] Such a good boy. I think he'll be all right now. Yep, me bones are achin', telling me that everything's gonna work out fine. [*To* NEVIL] Go, son! Score for Mum!
VOICE-OVER: He sidesteps Malley, passes to Hinch, to Grunta, Dooley finds a gap… He scores!

    BOOTY *grabs* NEVIL *in a bear hug.*

BOOTY: That's my boy. Always knew ya had it in ya, Nevil.
NEVIL: It's not Nevil.
BOOTY: What?
NEVIL: Call me Lucinda!

    The CROWD *gasp and look at each other.*

MAVIS: That's my boy. Always one for a joke.

    But MAVIS *looks uncertain.*

    Blackout.

THE END

GLOSSARY

bawl-baby	someone who cries easily
bungoo	money
'D's	detectives
galoot	fool
gammon laugh	insincere laugh
gungies	policemen
maryjawana	marijuana
snorters	policemen
sook	someone who cries easily
sool	to set off an attack
womba	crazy

Black Medea

Wesley Enoch

Wesley Enoch is the eldest son of Doug and Lyn Enoch, from Stradbroke Island. He has been Resident Director at Sydney Theatre Company, Artistic Director of Kooemba Jdarra Indigenous Performing Arts, and Ilbijerri Aboriginal and Torres Strait Islander Theatre; Associate Artist with Queensland Theatre Company; director of the Indigenous section of the 2006 Commonwealth Games Opening Ceremony; and Associate Artistic Director for Company B. As a writer, his work includes *The Sunshine Club, A Life of Grace and Piety, Grace, Cookie's Table* (Winner of the Patrick White Award 2006). Directing credits include *The Dreamers, Conversations with the Dead, Capricornia* (Company B, Belvoir St Theatre); *Stolen, Black Medea* (Playbox / Malthouse); *The Sunshine Club, The Cherry Pickers, Black-Ed Up, Black Medea, The 7 Stages of Grieving* (Sydney Theatre Company); *The Sapphires* (Melbourne Theatre Company); *Black-Ed Up, Radiance, The Sunshine Club, Fountains Beyond* (Queensland Theatre Company); *Murri Love, The 7 Stages of Grieving, The Dreamers, Changing Time, Purple Dreams, Bitin' Back* (Kooemba Jdarra); *Stolen, Shrunken Iris, Rainbow's End* and *Headhunter* (Ilbijerri).

Kyole Dungay as Child and Margaret Harvey as Medea in the Malthouse Theatre production of BLACK MEDEA, 2005. (Photo: Heidrun Löhr)

FIRST PERFORMANCE

Black Medea was first produced by Sydney Theatre Company's Blueprint at the Wharf 2 Theatre, Sydney, on 19 August 2000, with the following cast:

JASON	Nathan Ramsay
MEDEA	Tessa Rose
CHORUS	Justine Saunders
CHILD	Alex Frail/Kael Leahy

Director, Wesley Enoch
Designer, Stephanie Blake
Lighting Designer, Rachel Burke
Composer, Sarah de Jong
Dramaturg, Rachel Fennessey

The play was revived by Malthouse Theatre, Melbourne, and first performed at Belvoir St Theatre, Sydney, on 13 April 2005, with the following cast:

JASON	Aaron Pedersen
MEDEA	Margaret Harvey
CHORUS	Justine Saunders
CHILD	Kyole Dungay/Clive Cavanagh

Director, Wesley Enoch
Designer, Christina Smith
Lighting Designer, Rachel Burke
Sound Designer, Jethro Woodward

AUTHOR'S NOTE

Black Medea was the next piece I started to think about after *The 7 Stages of Grieving*. I was trying to mix the classical repertoire with the ability to tell contemporary stories. The power of a classic is that it can survive generations of interpretation and still be relevant to a modern time. Issues of love, violence, loyalty and betrayal are universal themes. I was inspired by the work of Cathy Craigie and in particular her play *Murri Love* which dealt with domestic violence. I felt that Aboriginal theatre must tackle big issues and find a depth of expression and spirit, and the classics was a way of doing it. I was invited to develop the concept in 2000, whilst I was Resident Director at the Sydney Theatre Company, to be staged at Wharf 2 Blueprints. A totally new production was worked up from this original and staged in 2005 at the Malthouse and Belvoir St.

Wesley Enoch

CHARACTERS

MEDEA
JASON, her husband
CHILD, their son
CHORUS

SECTION ONE

MEDEA WALKS IN THE DESERT

Blackout.

MEDEA *walks the perimeter of the space. A desert wind blows. The walls come alive. She winks in and out of sight as she walks. She glides as if by magic. She enters with her* CHILD. *She listens to the wind. She's concerned. She hugs her* CHILD *and sends him off.*

MEDEA'S BATTLE CRY

MEDEA: I am not frightened of you. I have faced everything I fear and defeated it. You think you are a match for me? The day has finally come… and today… I will vanquish you. Today… Jason and I will no longer run. And you will feel the sharpened edge of a mother's love and a wife's loyalty.

I can feel you, I can hear you coming. I am ready for you. Hear me… I am ready for you.

Come out and face me. Face me!

This is not a fit place for our final battle. But here you have chosen and here it must be. Were it up to me I would choose the open desert where you could not hide amongst these scared strangers clutching to the coast like cowering children.

I have not sacrificed everything to fail now. I have dreams.

Who am I to have such dreams? Who am I to go against even you?

I am a daughter of this Land, I have the knowledge of my people. I have the power of my clan, I have the strength of my marriage, I have the love of my husband, I have the weapons of my wits. I am Medea.

So come now and face me.

There is a blood debt to pay and not a drop of mine shall fall upon the thirsty earth.

JASON AND MEDEA 1

JASON *enters clutching his head, pursued by the wind.*

JASON: This fucking wind.
MEDEA: Did you close the door?
JASON: You think a man's a moron.
MEDEA: Jason…
JASON: Shut up for a while, will you…? Please.
MEDEA: I'll check the door.
JASON: The door's closed, the windows are shut, the whole fucking house is sealed.
MEDEA: I'll check it for you, love.
JASON: Don't leave me.
MEDEA: I'm just checking the door.
JASON: Stay here.
MEDEA: There's no wind, Jason.
JASON: I can hear it. Blowing like in the sails of a ship. Pushing me around.
MEDEA: There is no wind. It's still outside.
JASON: I'm telling you I can hear it.
MEDEA: It's in your head. Look at me, love… It's all in your head. Just don't let it in.
JASON: You think I'm crazy.
MEDEA: Jason…
JASON: [*to the wind*] Just shut the fuck up.
MEDEA: Shhh.

    A loud silence.

JASON: I'm not going out there tomorrow.
MEDEA: You'll feel better in the morning.
JASON: I'm not going.

    Pause.

MEDEA: Jason… did you get them to sign the contract?
JASON: No.
MEDEA: Jason my love… you have to get them to agree. We need them to sign.
JASON: It fell through. The deal's off.
MEDEA: No. It's not off. You get them to sign it tomorrow.

JASON: I told you it's over.
MEDEA: Look at me, my love. It's not over 'til we say it's over.
JASON: Let it go. It's gone.

Pause. Wind.

MEDEA: Your son needs new shoes.
JASON: We just bought a new pair.
MEDEA: And the school fees are overdue.
JASON: Pull him out of that school.
MEDEA: I'll see if they have a scholarship, shall I?
JASON: No fuckin' handouts!
MEDEA: Then… you have to ask your father for a loan.
JASON: Will you get off my back, for one second? A man just gets home and you have to be onto him about bills and shit. If you're that worried, go sell another painting.
MEDEA: No.
JASON: It puts food on the table, for fuck's sake.
MEDEA: All right, then. I'll put the food on the table, I'll pay the bills, I'll buy the shoes, I'll wear your fucking suit. [*Simultaneously with* JASON] Jason, talk to him. Say it's for his grandson.
JASON: [*simultaneously*] 'You call yourself a man and can't provide for your family.'
MEDEA: Then tell me what we should do?
JASON: I'm not talking to that cunt.
    Give a man a moment's peace to think.

The wind blows.

[*Whispering*] This fucking wind. It haunts me…
MEDEA: Don't let it in, you know where it's coming from…
JASON: Shut up with that shit.
MEDEA: Shut it out.
JASON: Fuck!
MEDEA: No regrets. That's what we said, we regret nothing. They'll sing you and you'll be lost. Block your ears, my love.
JASON: Shut up! It's you… I can hear you. You're the one. Shut your mouth.
MEDEA: They're singing you, Jason, they're making you crazy.
JASON: No more of your bullshit.
MEDEA: You can't take him… face me… leave him alone.

JASON: Shut up. Shut up. Shut up.

    I said shut up. It's you, Medea. Why don't you listen to me? Why do you keep going on? For fuck's sake… you make a man wild. Fuck!

    JASON *strikes* MEDEA.

    The lights change.

    MEDEA *lights some gum leaves and smokes out the kitchen.* JASON *sits on the floor. Head in his hands.*

BLACKOUT POEM 1

This Blackout Poem should be about establishing the family dynamics and the story.

JASON *and* MEDEA *dance together, kissing.*

CHILD *plays under the table.*

JASON *stands drunk in the house.*

MEDEA *is sitting at the table.*

CHILD *unwraps a birthday present.*

JASON *and* MEDEA *watch on.*

JASON *opens a fridge door, light pours out, takes out a bottle of beer.*

MEDEA *and* CHILD *huddle in a corner.*

JASON *throws the beer bottle, smashing it, and throws a chair.*

MEDEA *dances alone.*

CHILD *plays with the boat in the sand.*

JASON *sits alone at the table.*

MEDEA *picks up the chair.*

JASON *and* CHILD *play snap.*

MEDEA *and* JASON *stand with a suitcase.*

MEDEA *and* CHILD *stand with a suitcase.* CHILD *is wearing a suit jacket and men's shoes, he holds the boat.*

MEDEA *stands alone, she holds the boat.*

CHORUS *appears dressed as if coming from a long journey.*

SECTION TWO

CHORUS: G'day, you fellas. Tonight… we got to sing up this story for youse and we call upon the spirits of this Land and the people who have gone before us. We got to make it real but it doesn't mean it is real, we just got to think it is. You got to use your imagination now, bugger this TV shit, you got to work at it and listen. This story… it's like one of them stories you never want to tell 'cause it says we're all bad, that we got badness in us all. And I reckon we do, we battle it all the time. It's like that story that gets whispered in the corner 'cause no one wants to come out with it and say, 'Things have got to change'. No one wants to say, 'The grog's got to stop, the violence has got to stop, what we do to this country has got to stop'. Like being a warrior means being angry. But maybe being a warrior means being strong, knowing right from wrong and doing something about it.

But tonight you're witness, judge and jury… and we are the storytellers. It's one person's story but somehow it's about everyone. And this black woman she goes against everything that seems right… everything that seems proper… But that's what makes a story worth telling, doesn't it? So let's get on with it.

The heavens come alive.

THE TIME OF LOVE

JASON *and* MEDEA *dance together… they are sexual and intense.*

CHORUS: You've got to imagine a settlement on the edge of the desert, full of kids and dogs and nothing much else. A dusty corner of the world where the girls can't fall in love with a boy 'cause they're related and they have to get promised to a man, like in the old way. You got to imagine some of the girls sitting on the verandah of the canteen when the city men come in from the mine—then lining up to take their turn in the back seat of the company Toyota.

They say if you find yourself in this part of the world you're either running away from something or in search of it. No one thinks about marrying these blokes… maybe have a kid, but they don't expect him to hang around. So, if he's had a shit, shower and shave, he's in with a good chance.

The girls share around the one good dress, dance all Friday night 'til it's soaked in sweat, wash it the next morning, dry it in the midday sun... so some other girl can do it all again on the Saturday. And so it goes until the poor thing fades away, falling apart in the hands of a man.

But this man, he's different. He's a blackfella in a suit. Working his way up the corporate ladder, a city black with his hair wavy, bleached with saltwater air. Carrying his briefcase and jacket. Sweat marking his new shirt and his feet baking in his leather shoes. All the girls laugh at him.

But she's different, she has dreams of living in a big house with a garden, in a place where the sand doesn't creep in under the door. She's got her language, she knows her dances... but she's seen some of the world... the best education the gubbernment could afford... a school in a town with a uniform and French and unforgettable wealth... But she's come back... she's been promised to this fella with the right skin but she knows he's never going to get her what she wants. He's never going to get her out. So she's been waiting...

He wants to see the world,
She's been waiting to run away.

JASON *and* MEDEA *dance.*

Blackout.

He smells of soap and sweat.
She smells of ambition.

MEDEA'S DREAM

MEDEA *speaks to the audience.*

MEDEA: I had a dream. I dreamt I was staring into the desert and felt I would never be alone. In this dream my mother's standing there smiling, her hair playing in the wind. She doesn't say anything, she looks at me with a quiet smile. Beside her stands my grandmother. She looks just like my mother only she's got more history in her face. Her hair's tied back. This woman of law and language, standing ankle deep in the sand. Behind her another woman, looking at me,

I can see my reflection in her eyes. She looks familiar. Her skin's dark and weathered. Beside her another woman, and another and another, and then I can see an ocean of women stretching back out into the desert, stretching out to the horizon making the sand dark… standing facing me, looking to me.

SECTION THREE

JASON AND MEDEA 2

CHORUS: You know who I am. You know why I'm here.
MEDEA: Stop following us.
CHORUS: Stop running from me.
MEDEA: I am ready for you.
CHORUS: You are too outspoken, my girl.
MEDEA: Your advice is not welcome here.
CHORUS: My advice needs no invitation.
MEDEA: Get on with it.
CHORUS: Be careful of ambition. It blinds you… Where is your son?
MEDEA: He is not for you.
CHORUS: Where is he?
MEDEA: Out of your reach.

The CHILD *appears.*

Go play outside.
CHILD: Who is she?
MEDEA: No one you need to know. Go. Now!
CHORUS: This boy's got too much of his father in him.

CHORUS beckons CHILD *over. He goes to her, frightened.*

MEDEA: He is Jason's son.
CHORUS: He will be a strong young man.
MEDEA: Leave the boy alone.
CHORUS: [*to* CHILD] You don't belong here. It's time you came home. [*To* MEDEA] I seen what that man does. You got to come back to your family.
MEDEA: You know I'm not coming back.

CHORUS: There's just you and the boy.
> What have you done for the boy here? He's got no dance, no song, his uncles have never walked him through his country. For the father there's no way out. But for the boy… for you and the boy…

MEDEA: Jason will teach him everything he needs to know.

> CHORUS *laughs.*

We've never been stronger.

CHORUS: No. No… you can't see it, can you? You can't see how the love has gone sour, and how you tell yourself little lies… You think he'll change—'I can change him.' How he spends more time away. How you can't talk without fighting. How he never makes love to you. You can't see it… But you know in your heart, you can… you can see that he's been leaving you for a long, long time.

MEDEA: Get out of my house.

> CHORUS *lets go of* CHILD. *He runs to* MEDEA, *who holds him tight.*

CHORUS: Bring the boy back.

MEDEA: Get out.

CHORUS: Bring the boy back and all will be forgiven. Face us, face what you've done and all will be forgiven. We're waiting for you. Free the boy, before he becomes a copy of his father.

MEDEA: And if I don't?

CHORUS: Then I will unleash *hell* upon you.

> *The lights come down onto* MEDEA *sitting at the table.* JASON *enters into a shadow.*

MEDEA: Tell me it's all been worth it.

JASON: It's all been worth it.

MEDEA: Tell me you'll never leave me.

JASON: I'll never leave you.

MEDEA: Tell me you love me.
> Tell me you love me.

JASON: I love you.

MEDEA: Tell me you want me.
> Tell me you need me.
> Tell me how you need me.

SECTION FOUR

CHORUS: You've got to imagine back in the settlement on the edge of the desert the dogs and loveless girls, kids playing with sand but not knowing a beach. A dusty corner of the world where these two fell in love and how the other girls got cut. This strong woman of culture, with knowledge and beauty. A woman to fascinate his city friends, a trophy bride who could help him along his way. And how she saw her ticket out of there, a man equal to her ambitions, a man to have children who would one day rule the world.

    He promised her a star of her own. He took her in the sand dunes on a blanket in the night. There under the stars, in the desert they promised each other the kind of promises you make 'cause you can't imagine a world where they wouldn't be true.

MEDEA: I'll follow wherever you go. I'll walk with you and make a home in your shadow. I will regret nothing I do for you. I'll spill my own blood before I see a drop of yours. All you have to do is ask and I will make the desert bloom.

CHORUS: You got to imagine what her family thought, how they told her she was promised to the other bloke, how they reminded her of who she was and where she came from. How when they saw her pregnant belly, everything changed. You have to imagine how her father welcomed him into their house and fed him kangaroo tail and bush yams and called him son and forgave him. How they shared a drink and talked about the Landscape of their lives. How that night Jason watched the family dance and sing and felt the power of Medea.

BLACKOUT POEM 2

CHILD *is making a sand hill, he wrecks it.*

JASON *has a miner's hat on and looks at the cave.*

MEDEA *wipes down the table.*

JASON *is piggy-backing the* CHILD.

MEDEA *looks at the boat.*

JASON *and* CHILD *fix the boat.*

HE'S THINKING

CHORUS: He's thinking about his father, how he taught him to swim when he was five… throwing him in the deep end of the pool. Whenever he's scared he can taste chlorine.

He's thinking how his father would tell him stories of growing up eating fresh oysters off the rocks and swimming in the ocean. How he hates swimming.

He's thinking about how he can't close a deal, how he loses every job he gets by doing something stupid. Punching a man, not turning up, getting drunk.

How the wind haunts him.

He's thinking she should get out, leave him before she becomes just like his mother. How it's her fault.

He's thinking how simple it would be to live on the beach and eat fresh fish and prawns and mussels but he stinks of chlorine. He's thinking how he should teach his son to swim.

YOU DON'T NEED HER

CHORUS: What happened to you?

JASON: Who's there?

CHORUS: You used to be such a strong man.

JASON: Who are you?

CHORUS: You knew no fear. You used to travel everywhere… a leader of men… heading off to lands unknown…

JASON: Who's there?

CHORUS: Oh, the adventures you used to have. Oh, the life you used to have… But now…

JASON: Who are you?

CHORUS: I am your madness. I am your madness… from the mining.

Such a small price to pay.

She has robbed you of your youth and your spirit. She has taken everything you thought possible and dashed them on the rocks. Leave her.

CHORUS *runs her fingers through* JASON*'s hair.*

You don't need her.

JASON: I need her.

CHORUS: You know you don't need her. Wouldn't you like to feel the power of the ocean again?

    CHORUS *blows into his ear.*

JASON: That fucking wind.

CHORUS: I can stop all that. I can relieve you of your doubts. Leave her.

JASON: I can't leave her.

CHORUS: Leave her. She is the one causing the pain. She makes you carry the weight of her guilt. Her sin is piled high on your shoulders.

JASON: Medea is a good wife.

    Medea is a good mother.

CHORUS: And you are a good son. She's to blame.

    Now, leave her now before payback catches you. Cast her out.

JASON: I won't leave her.

CHORUS: You don't need her.

JASON: I do need her.

CHORUS: You need her to be like your mother.

JASON: What?!

CHORUS: You are becoming your father. You've learnt the lessons as your father did to his father, and you can't see that you're just the same.

JASON: I am not the same. I am not my father.

CHORUS: Your hair, your smile, your shoulders, eyes, skin, limbs, breath, light… And so the father becomes the son becomes the father becomes the son.

    CHORUS *kisses* JASON.

JASON: I love my son.

CHORUS: Then leave her.

JASON: I want a different life for him.

CHORUS: Then leave her.

JASON: I will not be like him.

CHORUS: Then leave her and you won't.

JASON: I have this memory of him screaming at me to let him in. Me… with my back pushing against the bedroom door. Mum huddled in the corner with the kids… Him… punching the door; his fist coming right through and as he pulls it back I can see the wood biting into his hand. There was so much blood. I washed the floor and walls. I couldn't wash the door. It frightened me.

CHORUS: Leave her and you won't become your father and he [*your son*] won't become you.

JASON AND MEDEA 3

MEDEA: Where would I go?
JASON: I don't care.
MEDEA: For how long?
JASON: Go back to your family.
MEDEA: And tell them you didn't want me…

    Silence.

Jason.
JASON: Tell 'em they were right. Tell 'em you're sorry. Tell them you'll marry that other bloke.
MEDEA: I chose you.
JASON: Go back where you belong.
MEDEA: Where? Where do I belong? I gave up belonging somewhere.
JASON: I didn't ask you to.
MEDEA: But I did.
JASON: I can survive without you.
MEDEA: All the dances and songs my granny taught me, that was my dowry. I bought your love, Jason.
JASON: I didn't ask you?
MEDEA: All the stories you used to impress your friends.
JASON: You signed your name. You wanted it.
MEDEA: I wanted you.
JASON: You wanted to get out of there.
MEDEA: I wanted you.
JASON: I never asked you to… [*give up anything*]
MEDEA: No, you asked me to betray—
JASON: [*overlapping*] That's enough!
MEDEA: You asked me to betray everything.
JASON: [*overlapping*] Stop!
MEDEA: As they turned up the bones of my ancestors.
    You saw how angry my father was… you heard the wailing of my aunties…
JASON: No… I couldn't hear over the sound of the bulldozers.
    I never asked you [*to do anything against your will*]—
MEDEA: You didn't have to ask. I did it freely, 'cause I love you.
JASON: It's over.
MEDEA: *No!* I refuse.

JASON: You can't stay with me...
MEDEA: With you...
JASON: You used me. You're always wanting more, you're never happy, never happy with what you got. Now I got nothing more to give you... Go back, crawl back and beg forgiveness.
MEDEA: I've sacrificed for you.
JASON: And what've you got to show for it?
MEDEA: A home, a husband, a son.
JASON: You still have a son.
MEDEA: Where will I go, Jason?
JASON: No more.
MEDEA: When I go down the street people stare at me. Whitefellas, blackfellas. They know I'm from somewhere they've never been... and they're scared. I remind them of what they don't have. They walk around like they're scared to put a foot wrong, apologising with every step—too scared to admit it, admit they don't belong here. I've known the spirits to come up through my feet and take my body when I'm dancing. That's who you fell in love with.

    MEDEA *lets sand run through her fingers.*

    Silence.

Let's go back to the mine and face it together. Pack up, just us. How it used to be. The money was good, you loved me. We just forget about this... we don't have to talk about it, we can forget about it, we can forget the whole thing...

    Who is it? I want to know. Is she pretty? Say something!

    What's she got that I haven't? We promised each other—
JASON: Stop the bullshit!
MEDEA: I promised to the spirits.
JASON: It's over.
MEDEA: They'll come for you—
JASON: There are no spirits. You're talking to your fucking self.
MEDEA: You're wrong.
JASON: You're going mad.
MEDEA: We can go to the ocean again—
JASON: Shut up!
MEDEA: You can get a job—

    JASON *reacts violently and throws* MEDEA *to the ground.*

JASON: Are the spirits talking to you now? Can you hear them? Are they telling you anything? What are they saying? They're telling you it's over... They're telling you to stay the fuck away from me!

SHE'S THINKING

CHORUS: You think... she's telling herself that she should've kept her mouth shut. That she should know by now, that she can read his moods and forecast them like the weather.

You think... she's telling herself how she deserved it, she shouldn't have said... whatever it was... he'll need time to cool down. He'll come back, he always does... he'll say sorry and she'll forgive him... she always does.

You're worried... what the neighbours heard and what she'll tell them.

What she'll say if they ask... they never ask.

How she misses the woman she was meant to be.

No... she's not thinking these things.

MEDEA PRAYS

MEDEA *sits with a cup of tea. The sound of wind.*

MEDEA: A loveless bed, the madness, a man—a shell of everything he was capable of, that's what you've left me. You have taken any peace I dreamed possible. You have driven him away from me. I have known the riches of the whiteman's world but you have shown me poverty of the spirit. I gave up a father, a brother, a mother, a country, I led him to sacred places, I turned my back when they dug up the earth...

I have no choice. In crime I have gained my home, in crime I must leave it.

I'll take what's mine. I gave him all the happiness he has, I gave him a home, I gave him a son. I gave him my life, I want a life in return. You have witnessed everything in this Land, you've been here long before Jason and Medea and you'll be here long after what I do tonight. I have sinned against all that was sacred.

Do not judge me, for tonight I am coming home, an outcast.

JASON'S DREAM

JASON: I had this dream. I'm following this man... I can't see his face but I know it's my father. I'm following him down this alley between two high walls... There are no doors or windows but I can hear other people. I can hear the ocean somewhere outside. The wind's howling.

The alley's only wide enough for one... I'm following my father and I can see we're in a line of men all walking in the same direction down this thin alley. Then we stop like we reached the end.

I'm staring into the back of my father's head and I look up. The sun's burning the back of my eyes... I look back down... and I see my father's face... He's now facing me... there's anger in his eyes... I turn around to face the other direction and see the empty alley stretching out to the horizon and I realise I have to lead the line... I have to take the first step in the new direction but I can't... In front of me, I see my son... he's looking straight ahead with no one in front of him... I can hear him crying. I want to take him by the hand... I want to show him a way out... but I can't show him anything... so I put my hands on his shoulders and shove him to start walking.

CHORUS: Back in a dusty corner of time when young love was possible. You have to imagine ambition taking shape... before the winds of the desert blew with intent. This couple see a way of escaping... see a way of making the life they want. She carries his child and hatches plots and intrigues like a true survivor of the desert. Between the blood-money bonuses and mining royalties she can lay the map for their success.

The spirits have led me to this place, Jason. Here I know our future is made. Under this mound is the largest vein of that which you mine, here the stories tell us the Great Spirit lay down leaving its breath in the rocks. Here where we bury our dead in the trees and in the earth. Here among the bones of the dead lay our future. This is what you must do... this is what you must do to plan our escape.

An unwilling Jason is convinced in the name of his unborn child, in the name of the riches the white world promised. She screams madness to him... for what sane man would rape his mother?

BLACKOUT POEM 3

JASON *holds a toy bulldozer box.*
CHILD *with bulldozer.*
MEDEA *is banging her head up against the leg of the table.*

JASON *and* CHILD *arm wrestle.*
MEDEA *is banging her head up against the leg of the table.*

CHILD *pulls a bottle of beer out of the fridge.*
JASON *teaches* CHILD *to box.*
MEDEA *is banging her head up against the leg of the table.*

JASON AND MEDEA 4

MEDEA *carries an iron pipe.* JASON *is asleep at the table, a bottle of beer beside him.*

MEDEA: Once will be enough… That'll be my revenge.
   He won't know what's happened. He just won't wake up.

   MEDEA *goes to strike* JASON *but stops herself.*
   The CHILD *is watching with the boat. She looks to him.*

CHILD: Mum…
MEDEA: Go back to bed.
CHILD: I can't sleep.
MEDEA: Come here.

   MEDEA *puts the pipe down and puts* CHILD *on a chair.*

   We're going away, just you and me. We're going to see the desert…

   CHILD *looks confused.*

   A desert is like a beach. You'd love that…
CHILD: Isn't Daddy coming?
MEDEA: 'Course he's coming. He'll be joining us later. I want you to go pack some clothes.
CHILD: When are we be coming back?
MEDEA: Go pack your clothes.
CHILD: I don't want to go.

MEDEA: Shhh. Do as you're told. Go now.

She indicates for him to go quietly.

JASON: The boy's not going with you.

MEDEA: We're leaving.

JASON: He's not going.

MEDEA: Come and visit if you want.

JASON: He's staying with me.

MEDEA: You and the next slut you move in here.

MEDEA *stands, revealing the pipe.*

JASON: He's my son. Are you going to use that?

MEDEA: I'm taking the boy home. Back to his people, so he can grow up with dignity.

JASON: He's my flesh and blood. I'll teach him everything he needs to know.

MEDEA: I carried him. I gave birth to him. I nursed him when he was sick. He sucked milk from my breast. What can you give him?

JASON: A son belongs with his father. Take what you want but you're leaving the boy.

MEDEA: There's nothing more I want.

JASON: Better for you to take my life, to rip out my heart.

MEDEA: Then give it to me… give me your heart. Give me what you promised me, give me a life.

CHILD: Mum.

JASON *takes the pipe away from her. He wrestles her to the table.*

JASON: I want you gone, do you understand…? You will not be taking the boy… Promise me… on everything you hold sacred, the boy will not leave this house… Promise me… promise me… If you take that fuckin' boy, I'll track you down to the ends of the earth and beat your fuckin' brains out… Go to bed.

MEDEA CURSES

MEDEA: Give me a hair and a fingernail and I will curse you, Jason. Something with your sweat and I will curse you. Everything you have done to me, come back to haunt you ten times bigger. I want you to feel empty. The kind of emptiness I feel without you. I want you to wake up every morning and feel a part of you is missing. I want you to search and everywhere you look to see me... whenever you close your eyes to see me. Let the spirits hear me curse... let everything you love hurt you. Wherever love is inside you let it cause you pain, from the sharp hard jabs to weeping bedsores.

Let every time you love be like a knife between your ribs. Let no type of love be safe from my curse, not the love of a woman nor the love of a son.

I want you alive, I want you to feel an emptiness for as long as you live. I want you to carry the torment to your deathbed, alone and unloved. I want you to regret your life and when you die I will separate your bones and speak your name, and force your spirit to wander aimless without a home.

My revenge is born, already born, for I have given birth.

CHILD *enters.*

Shhhh.

MEDEA'S VISITOR

CHORUS: The Land reclaims you. In the end we will always welcome you back. When we won't say your name and bury your body to rot for a year, the Land will reclaim you.

When we have performed the rites, when we have burnt the flesh from your bones and painted them with red ochre. We'll wrap your bones in bark and wail for your body and then you'll know... you can't really leave your Land.

CHORUS *speaks to* CHILD.

She reckons she left it behind with her family, left it behind like a footprint and every time she walks on foreign soil that foot speaks to her telling her it has a memory of where it belonged. You're related to the sand dunes and the waterholes. You belong in your Land. The Land will always reclaim you.

MEDEA AND THE CHILD

MEDEA: Spirits, this is my son. I have failed him. He has never known his Land, never left a footprint. I have abandoned him to follow his father. I have kept from him his songs and dances. I have denied him his family. Though he has tasted the spirit from my breast I have refused him his place in the Land. I've gone mad with living in two worlds.

In this long dark night I see it clearly—if he stays, he will become a copy of his father. He will grow up bruising the ones he loves, his children will live in fear, he will be another wandering soul. A mother's love will not allow it.

Spirits, the moon pulls me like the tide, I will not allow the sun to rise for him another day in this house. Before this night is through, my son will be freed, before the next day dawns, my son will know the spirits of his Land. I will take him.

Tonight I'm coming home. Let no man stand in my way.

SAND PAINTING

CHORUS: When my time comes burn me
Take my bones and colour them red
Wrap them in the bark of a tree
And hang me where I can curse.

When my time comes watch for me
For I have learnt to stone my heart,
Learnt to put aside my joy
For some other life.

When my time comes I will wait for you
In the secret place with all your fears
And I shall scream, to shatter
Any peace you have.

When this time comes you will see
The strength that I have never shown
And I will blow a whispered wind
To send you mad.

When my time comes let it be known
That I have loved.
That I acted
With the only strength I had.

Now my time has come
And, friends, am weary
From all the struggle
That brings us together.

When my time comes burn me
Take my bones and colour them red
Wrap them in the bark of a tree
And hang me where I can curse.

SACRIFICE

MEDEA *takes* CHILD *by the hand and leads him to the sink. She runs the tap. She washes* CHILD *and takes him to the table. She lays him to sleep. She takes the pipe and beats him to death.*

JASON AND MEDEA 5

JASON: What have you done? What have you done?

MEDEA: Look upon this sight, Jason... and weep. Even in vengeance I am faithful to you. Here is your son. Here is my flesh and blood. You are cursed. I have saved him from becoming you. And if in my womb another of your children lies waiting, know this... that he will encounter the same fate as his brother. Look at me. Let my face be tattooed in your brain for I have done the rites and this house must burn to honour our son. Look at me and see the last face that loved you. I have left you. The spirits call me back to my home... Whatever my hell, I will sleep pleased in the knowledge that my grief has yours as company. Wherever you go, bear witness that there are no gods.

> MEDEA *burns down the house.* JASON *carries the body of* CHILD *offstage.*

THE DESERT STORY

The sound of the desert wind.

CHORUS: She's walking in the desert... alone... She walks, her feet are stained red. She's barely alive, one breast hangs out abandoned.

She holds a package close to her… a broken boat. She doesn't cry, she's cried enough. Her lips are cracked, her dark skin blistered. She makes her way over the dunes, winking out of sight then appearing again at the next crest. She walks in a straight line tracking across the sand. She's close to death, everything about her dry…

She whispers as she walks, singing up the desert. The sand stretches out in all directions… She sings up the wind… and she is no more.

MEDEA *disappears and becomes the wind.*

THE END

King Hit

David Milroy and Geoffrey Narkle

Geoffrey Narkle was born in Narrogin, Western Australia, in April 1951. In 1997, he co-wrote *King Hit* with David Milroy, which chronicled his own life from mission kid to manhood, travelling throughout Western Australia as part of Stewart's boxing troupe where he was known as the Barker Bulldog. In 1993 he became a pastor at the Aboriginal Evangelical Church, Balga, and was a very respected and strong presence in the Noongar community. He was married to Glenys Narkle and they had four children: Bradley, Geoff Jnr, Vanessa and Melanie. Geoffrey Narkle died in August 2005.

For David Milroy's biography, see the title page for *Windmill Baby*.

Lynley Tubb and Derek Nannup in the Yirra Yaakin production of KING HIT, at the Dolphin Theatre, Nedlands, 1997. (Photo: David Dare Parker)

FIRST PERFORMANCE

King Hit was first produced by Yirra Yaakin Theatre Company at the Dolphin Theatre, Nedlands, on 23 October 1997, with the following cast:

    Warren Collard
    Derek Nannup
    James Sollis
    Lynley Tubb

Director, David Milroy
Designer, Michael Betts
Costume Designer, Ron Gidgup
Lighting Designer, Linda Haywood
Musical Director, David Chesson

AUTHOR'S NOTE

King Hit for me was a realisation that I carried the pain of the Stolen Generations with me. The reality of losing my family bond—and the searching for who I was—came to the point where I just had to do something. I've seen too many brothers and sisters die, seen the effects of being taken away impact across generations and I had to force myself to take the first step towards healing. It made me aware that it's all right to talk, to seek out positive ways of dealing with pain and to push forward with a meaningful life. I've managed to find a spiritual centre, both through culture and my belief in God and it's helped me forgive myself for the hate I've carried, the loss I've felt and the turmoil I've raised up from. I cried all the way through *King Hit*—tears of joy, tears of pain and in sharing my story with you, I share my appreciation of life.

Geoffrey Narkle, 2002

CHARACTERS

GEOFF

CAROLINE, his sister
LARGY, his father
BELLA, his mother
CHARLIE, his cousin, a boxer
AUNTY
UNCLE

GEORGE
KID DYNAMITE, a boxer

DALE
JACKIE
KERRY
NOONG

TRADER
SCHOOL HEAD
JUDGE
POLICE
FATHER LUMEN
MISSION PRIEST
WELFARE OFFICER

ASSORTED BOYS, GIRLS, MEN, WOMEN, FRIENDS, CROWD, MOB

KID DYNAMITE *and* GEORGE *enter.* KID *beats a drum and as* GEORGE *begins spruiking a crowd gathers.*

GEORGE: Holda! Holda! Holda! There's gonna be a fight in this house! There's gonna be a fight in this house! Come and see my fighters, come and see my champions! They're the best in the land, they'll fight any man! Rally the bells and the drums. We'll fight any man— black, white, blue or brindle. If you've got the courage to come and have a dash then you get the cash. Do we have any takers? Do we have any takers?

GEOFF: Your fighters are a mob of pussycats!

GEORGE: Holda! Holda! Holda! Hello, hello, hello! Here's the little troublemaker. Follows me from town to town, ladies and gentlemen. Don't come around here looking for trouble!

  AUNTY *comes forward.*

GEOFF: Your fighters are a mob of pussycats and Kid Dynamite's the biggest!

AUNTY: You tell 'em, neph!

GEORGE: Had to leave the troop, ladies and gentlemen, 'cause he was too jealous of Kid Dynamite winning all the fights.

GEOFF: I'm the best fighter you ever had!

GIRL: Yeah. He's Moorditj!

AUNTY: You keep your hands off my nephew!

GEORGE: If you've got a grudge to settle, Bulldog, then step into the ring. Kid Dynamite will blow you apart and smash you to smithereens.

GIRL: Make 'im jump, Geoffery!

  GEOFF *shirtfronts* KID DYNAMITE.

GEOFF: I'll fight Kid Pussycat and you'll wish you never crossed the Barker Bulldog.

GEORGE: Tough words, ladies and gentlemen. Let's see how tough he is in the tent. Come inside and see Kid Dynamite and the Barker Bulldog settle this grudge match once and for all.

AUNTY: I'm comin' in, that's my nephew!

GIRL: Me too! He solid, eh!

GEORGE: There's gonna be a fight in this house! There's gonna be a fight in this house! We fight by the Marquess of Queensbury rules, *no* rabbit punching, *no* hitting below the belt and *no* king hits! Keep it clean, boys, keep it clean! Touch gloves and come out fighting. Keep it clean, Bulldog!

> GEOFF *and* DYNAMITE *gee fight—a staged fight to keep the* CROWD *entertained.*

GEOFF: Where'd ya get your pretty belt buckle from, ya girlfriend?
KID: Barker Bulldog, all bark and no bite.
GEORGE: Let me check your gloves. Now fight!
AUNTY: Watch out, Geoffrey!

> GEOFF *gets king hit.*

Get up, Geoff! Come on, get up.
GEORGE: … 7, 8, 9, 10!
GIRL: Hope you didn't bust his pretty nose.
GEORGE: Well, there you go, ladies and gentlemen!
GEOFF: I'm not finished yet!

> GEORGE *moves to* GEOFF, *takes off his gloves and pushes them into his chest.*

GEORGE: Nothing but a troublemaker, nothing but a troublemaker, nothing but a troublemaker…

> BELLA *walks to the front of the stage, bends down and looks at the sand.* LARGY *walks up behind her, placing his hand on her shoulders.*

BELLA: My babies, Largy! My babies!
LARGY: Come on, Bella, they're gone. There's nothing we can do.
GEOFF: [*to the audience*] That used to be me. The Barker Bulldog boxing for Stewart's troupe. When I decided to share my story and write this play I travelled back to the reserve where I was born. As I walked to the top of the Granite Ridge a small flock of black cockatoos welcomed me back to Clayton Road Reserve. When I was a little fella I stood on this ridge looking out at the farms spread out like a patchwork quilt. To the east about a mile away was the town of Narrogin. That's where the Wadjullas lived. Noongar's lived on the reserve fenced in by the rubbish tip, a farmer's barbed-

wire fence and Clayton Road. At the entrance to the reserve was a big white sign.

ACTORS: 'No whites, no alcohol and no taking Aboriginal women.'

GEOFF: [*to the audience*] Old man Abram had his camp to the west of the reserve on the rise. From there he could keep an eye on everyone. His camp was the same as ours and everyone else's. Tar drums, canvas, bits of tin and anything else that we could find on the tip. He never spoke much English, even his cocky spoke Noongar. The first Noongar word I learnt was from that cocky. When the police turned up at night with their spotlights the cocky would screech out, 'Manatj! Manatj!' Noongars weren't allowed to be out after dark and when the sun went down Mum would start worrying.

BELLA: Geoffrey! Caroline! Largy, go see where them kids are, it's getting dark.

LARGY: Ah! Don't worry about them, nowhere to go around here.

BELLA: Well, tell 'em to come home before that rat ban comes around with its spotlight. Geoffrey took some damper down to old man Abram's camp.

LARGY: Haw, that boy! Any excuse to hear that cocky talk. Here they come now! Worrying about nothing.

GEOFF and his sister CAROLINE come racing on.

CAROLINE: Mum! The cocky taught Geoff another word.

GEOFF: Shut up, Caroline!

CAROLINE: He taught Geoffery to say…

She whispers.

BELLA: Geoffery! That cocky's gonna wind up in a stew if he keeps talking like that.

LARGY: Settle down, it's not the cocky's fault.

BELLA: Go an' get cleaned up, you two.

CAROLINE: I told you it was a rude word.

GEOFF and CAROLINE leave.

LARGY: Saw Mr Fowler today.

BELLA: And?

LARGY: He reckons he's got three months work clearing and burning.

BELLA: And how much is he gonna pay ya?

LARGY: Not a lot, but it will get us off the reserve for a while. All I need is permission from Native Welfare.

BELLA: You're not getting any younger, Largy. You're breaking your back just for rations.

LARGY: I can't just sit around on the reserve every day.

BELLA But when we come back we're worse off. No money and just startin' over again.

LARGY: They're getting a good price for possum skins. You can tan some and when the work's finished we can trade them for some clothes for the kids and I'll buy a new hat like we seen on that movie poster and... let me think... a pretty new dress for you.

BELLA: Go away, Largy! Don't start making promises! Don't start making promises.

> LARGY *and* BELLA *kneel and tan possum skins.* GEOFF *and* CAROLINE *watch them at work.*

GEOFF: [*to the audience*] At night our camp would be filled with the smell of fires smouldering in the winter rains. I'd curl up in my Native Welfare blanket and watch Mum and Dad get the skins ready for tanning. Any scraps of meat would be snapped up by our two kangaroo dogs that we used for hunting.

LARGY: I reckon this skin will buy pretty ribbons for the girls and this one a new pair of pants for Geoffery.

CAROLINE: Why don't you make him a pair out of a kangaroo skin?

GEOFF: Why don't we make your ribbons out of kangaroo guts?

BELLA: Geoffery!

LARGY: Go to sleep, you two.

GEOFF: [*to the audience*] Dad would work from sun-up to sundown clearing and burning the land and when it was all finished we headed back to the reserve. Not with too much money, but a lot of possum skins.

> TRADER *enters.*

LARGY: Gorn, get out of here.

TRADER: By gee! What's your secret, Largy, I never seen so many skins?

LARGY: We've been clearing land at Fowlers. Biggest mob of Coomall.

BELLA: Give me a hand with these skins, Geoffrey. Largy, take this medicine to your mum, she hasn't been too well lately.

LARGY: Okay! But you make sure you pick a real pretty dress, as good as a Wadjulla's.
TRADER: Thought you would have traded these in town by now.
BELLA: You know we don't like going into town. Went to buy some medicine for Grandma Hilda yesterday. I had to wait an hour while all the Wadjullas got served first.
TRADER: Well, I'll take anyone's money. All business is good business.

BELLA *holds a dress up against her.* TRADER *exits.*

BELLA: What you reckon, Geoffrey! Think ya dad will like this one?
GEOFF: It's pretty, Mum, pretty as paint!
CAROLINE: Look at my ribbons, Daddy. Am I pretty as paint?

LARGY *enters with his head down.*

BELLA: Here, Largy, what do you think of this one…? What's wrong, Largy?

BELLA *crouches and wails.* LARGY *stands with head down.*

GEOFF: [*to the audience*] That night I woke up to the sound of wailing. Mum and Dad were gone, so I followed the sound down to where Grandma's camp was. Her body had been wrapped in a blanket and laid by the fire. My aunties were kneeling next to her and wailing so loudly I became scared. So I held onto my father's leg. It was the first time I had seen him cry and the last time I heard the wailing of Noongar women.
LARGY: I was talking to Mr Fowler today. He says the Native Welfare are moving us to a bigger reserve at Coolballing Road.
BELLA: Nice of Native Welfare to tell us. I suppose we'll find out when the bulldozers turn up and they load us onto the back of a cattle truck.
LARGY: Couldn't be any worse than this place. He reckons there's going to be houses and a toilet block with showers and all.
BELLA: I suppose we get to keep the police patrols and everyone locked up after dark.
LARGY: Aagh! We'll be able to come and go as we want. We'll be as good as white people.
GEOFF: We gonna be white, Dad?
CAROLINE: They gonna paint us?
BELLA: You all right, Largy?
LARGY: You know all the work I've been doing for Mr Fowler?

BELLA: Keep goin'!

LARGY: Well, he said he'd write a letter on my behalf to the Native Welfare Department and that should help me get my citizenship papers.

BELLA: Citizenship papers?

LARGY: I'll be as good as any white man and you and the kids will be citizens as well.

BELLA: Largy, listen to me, even if you stick that citizenship paper to your forehead, Wadjullas are still gonna treat you the same.

LARGY: I'll be able to travel to other towns to get work. I won't have to get permission from Native Welfare. You know I'm a gun shearer, we can make a good life for our kids. Coolballing Road Reserve is gonna be a new start for us, hey kids.

CAROLINE: I don't want to get painted.

BELLA: A piece of paper's gonna make no difference.

LARGY: When I get my papers you're putting on that pretty dress, and we're gonna walk down the main street of Narrogin like we own it.

BELLA, LARGY and UNCLE set up for a game of two-up (stylised).

GEOFF: [*to the audience*] Well, it wasn't long before the government moved us to our brand new reserve at Coolballing Road. We'd burn tyres for light and all the kids would play chasey 'til the rat ban showed up with its spotlight. Then we'd run to our shacks, we'd call pigpens and listen to the older boys playing cat and mouse with the police. During shearing season there was plenty of money on the reserve. When they started piling up the tyres we knew tonight the pennies would be flying.

LARGY spins two-up coins with party music in the background.

UNCLE: Send 'em down, Largy!

LARGY: Yukeye!

The coins hit the ground.

Aagh!

BELLA: Come on, Largy, you can do better than that.

UNCLE: You might be a gun shearer, Largy, but you're not too gun at tossing the coins.

BELLA: Don't listen to your uncle, he's just trying to put you off. I set you five pounds he tails it.

UNCLE: I'll take your money.

BELLA: Come on, Largy, set 'em up.
UNCLE: Throw 'em up, Largy.

    LARGY *tosses the coins again.*

LARGY: Hey, Geoffrey, stop playing with that dog, you're supposed to be looking out for Manatj.

    UNCLE *tries to sneak away.*

CAROLINE: Mum, Billy's chasing me with a goanna.
BELLA: Billy, I'll chase you with a stick if you don't put that caarda down!
LARGY: Hey, Unc! Where you going? Come on now, pay up!

    UNCLE *gives some money to* BELLA, *she signals for more. The stylised two-up action continues during* GEOFF*'s speech.*

GEOFF: [*to the audience*] We used to have a dog on the reserve called Two-Up. When the coins went up in the air he'd run around and around the stump. By the end of the night the trench was that deep you couldn't see him. One night Billy found a goanna and when all the money was laid down and the pennies were flying through the air he threw the goanna in just as the pennies hit the ground.
BELLA: I'm gonna flog you for this, Billy!
GEOFF: All hell broke loose as they chased him off into the darkness. All that was left behind was the money and Two-Up still running around that stump.

    LARGY *enters.*

LARGY: Where's the kids?
BELLA: They're playing down at the creek.

    LARGY *whistles to* GEOFF.

LARGY: Geoffrey! C'mon, Bella, let's get them cleaned up.
BELLA: What for?
LARGY: You still got that pretty dress?
BELLA: Yeah!
LARGY: Well, put it on!
BELLA: What's goin' on, Largy?
LARGY: Mr Fowler's letter did the trick… I got my dog licence.
BELLA: Your citizenship papers.
LARGY: Yep. You got some glue?

BELLA: What for?

LARGY: So I can stick it to my forehead. C'mon, were going to the pictures.

> LARGY *and* BELLA *walk arm-in-arm down the street with* GEOFF *behind. A* WHITE MAN *walks past and* BELLA *and* LARGY *step aside to let him pass.*

One day we won't have to get off the footpath to let them pass.

BELLA: Come on, Largy, we'll be late for the pictures.

> LARGY *walks up to buy tickets off the* MAN.

LARGY: Three tickets, please.

MAN: First three rows are for blacks and, don't forget, leave the theatre… after the white folks have left.

GEOFF: [*to the audience*] We had to watch the movie looking straight up at the screen but once the movie started I'd drift into a world far away from Narrogin. Noongars fell in love with Elvis and if there was any way we could have claimed him for a relation we would have. The only time I seen Wadjullas having a good time with Noongars was when we saw *Jailhouse Rock*.

> *The actors start to dance to the sound of Elvis Presley's 'Jailhouse Rock'.*

Noongars couldn't stay in their seats. Wadjullas were shocked. They started dancing in the aisles. But Elvis was the king. Before you knew it we were all dancing together.

> *The music ends. As the dancers stop they end up in a line across the back of the stage.*

Not long after, I started school and I soon learnt every word a Noongar could be called.

ACTOR 1: Abo.

ACTOR 2: Nigger.

ACTOR 3: Boong.

> GEOFF *shrugs it off.* CAROLINE *appears.*

CAROLINE: Geoffrey, Dad's here!

GEOFF: What?

CAROLINE: He's been helping the Wadjullas in the canteen.

> *The* SCHOOL HEAD.

HEAD: Well, thank you, Mr... err...
LARGY: Narkle, Largy Narkle.
HEAD: Well, thank you, Mr Narkle, for helping out. I'm sure you're a very busy man.
LARGY: Nah, I'm free all this week. I'll see you tomorrow... Mr... err ...
HEAD: Wallace... err... Mr Wallace.

  LARGY spots GEOFF and CAROLINE.

LARGY: Close your mouth! You're as bad as those womans in the canteen. Now you come straight home from school.
GEOFF: [*to the audience*] Dad turned up every day that week just to show them how proud he was of us kids. By the end of the week he was calling all the Wadjullas by their first name.
LARGY: Bob, Trev... Johnno!
GEOFF: [*to the audience*] And somehow school seemed a happier place.

  A BOY *is looking through the window of an empty Wudjulla's house.*

BOY: Hey, Geoffrey? Look here!
GEOFF: Choo, Gary! You shouldn't be looking in a whitefella's house.
BOY: It's empty, they must have moved out while it's getting painted.
GEOFF: Haw, boy! Look at the carpet. I betcha Elvis lives in a house like this.
BOY: Come on! The window's open, let's finish off the painting.

  The boys mime painting. Another boy has been acting as COCKY *(a lookout).*

COCKY: Manatj! Manatj!
GEOFF: [*to the audience*] I'd never been in trouble with the police before and going to court was the scariest day of my life. I'd never seen Mum and Dad look so worried. They did their best to dress me up and told me to talk politely to the judge and answer him if he asked me questions. But as I sat listening to him I didn't really understand a word he was saying.

  The JUDGE *is questioning a* POLICE OFFICER.

JUDGE: Character and conduct of child up to the present?
POLICE: Good, Your Honour.
JUDGE: Character of parents?
POLICE: Good, Your Honour.

JUDGE: Present offence.
POLICE: Section 80 of the Police Act, wilfully spoiling a dwelling with paint.
JUDGE: And what is the opinion of the Department?
POLICE: It is the Department's opinion that this lad is easily led but we do not anticipate any further trouble.
JUDGE: Hmm! This is a serious offence, my boy, what do you have to say for yourself?
GEOFF: I'm a good boy at school.
JUDGE: Hmm! And I would warn the parents to exercise greater control over the lad. Otherwise action will be taken. Dismissed under Section 26 of the Child Welfare Act. Restitution by father: five pounds.
GEOFF: [*to the audience*] Five pounds was a lot of money and Dad had to do a lot of shearing to pay off the fine. But because Dad had citizenship he could move around the district freely to find work. He needed transport so he brought an old T-Model Ford. [*Young GEOFF to LARGY*] You gonna take us for a ride, Dad?
BELLA: [*entering*] Yer, you kids go with him. Your dad needs someone to stop him from killin' himself.
GEOFF: Why, Mum?
BELLA: Well, he was driving along good, goes like this, and he must been daydreaming about the old days, 'cause when he pulled up to Mr Fowler's gate in his Blackfellas' Cadillac he thought he was on a horse.
LARGY: You promised you wouldn't say anything.
BELLA: I never promised nothing.
GEOFF: What happened?
BELLA: Next minute he was pulling on the steering wheel like they were reins and shouting, 'Whoa! Whoa!' and 'Whaakitch!' Knocked the gate right off the hinges.
LARGY: You know I've been riding horses all my life.
BELLA: You'll be putting oats in the fuel tank next.
LARGY: All right! You had your laugh, but just remember that Blackfellas' Cadillac is taking us to Perth for your aunty's funeral.
BELLA: All right, Largy, but hey, give it a good drink before we go.
GEOFF: [*to the audience*] My older brother Greg and his wife Loma had been moved from the reserve into a transitional house at Granite Road.

LARGY *cranks the car but it doesn't start.*

LARGY: Come on, Bella, put ya foot down.

GEOFF: [*to the audience*] If they could live like whitefellas there was a chance of them getting a house in town.

LARGY *cranks the car again and it starts.*

LARGY: That's him! We'll only be a couple of days, Greg.

BELLA: Make sure you wear your shoes.

LARGY: The funeral's on Thursday.

BELLA: Come straight home from school.

LARGY: Come on, Bella, this car doesn't run on fresh air, you know.

BELLA: And help Loma around the house.

LARGY: Stop fussin', we'll be back in a few days.

BELLA: All right! All right! I'm comin'. He's getting as cranky as his old car.

LARGY: If you kids are good we'll bring you back a present from Perth.

LARGY *and* BELLA *go off.* GEOFF *and* CAROLINE *sit playing knucklebones.*

GEOFF: [*to the audience*] We were all missing Mum and Dad, especially my baby sister Caroline. But Greg and Loma took good care of us and we felt pretty flash living in a transitional house. I'd come straight home from school and played out the back with my three sisters.

GEOFF *and* CAROLINE *still playing knucklebones.*

ACTOR 1: Form to accompany Mandate of Committal of Award. Health of family?

ACTOR 2: Good, Your Honour.

ACTOR 1: Locality of home?

ACTOR 2: Coolballing Road Reserve, Narrogin.

ACTOR 1: Favourable or unfavourable?

ACTOR 2: Favourable, Your Honour.

ACTOR 1: Type of house?

ACTOR 2: Wooden, two-room cottage in good state of repair.

ACTOR 1: Sleeping arrangements?

ACTOR 2: Two beds for four children.

ACTOR 1: Cleanliness?

ACTOR 2: Very clean, Your Honour.

ACTOR 1: Are home conditions adequate for a child's needs?
ACTOR 2: Yes, Your Honour.
ACTOR 1: Attitude of children to school work?
ACTOR 2: In each case children are interested.
ACTOR 1: Previous court appearances?
ACTOR 2: Geoffrey, wilfully spoiling a dwelling with paint. It appears the parents do not demonstrate any control over their children.
ACTOR 1: What is the opinion of the Department?
ACTOR 2: Another case of delinquent parents and very adult ones at that. They have a good set of circumstances. A nice home, income and lovely children. Unfortunately they are not fit to have children.
ACTOR 1: The court decision is for the children to be committed to the Child Welfare Department until eighteen years of age and to be placed in Wandering Mission. Next.
GEOFF: [*to the audience*] We were playing out the back as the car pulled up at the front. It wasn't too much longer when Loma asked us to come inside. She was crying and my brother stood still with his head down. When the man told us we were going to live on a mission my sisters started crying and calling out for Loma. He told them to sit in the back seat and me in the front. As we drove off I stared at the front door of my brother's house hoping he'd grab us out of the car.

A local BOY *comes up to* GEOFF.

BOY: Hey, Geoffrey? What you doin' in a whitefella's car?
GEOFF: We're going to a mission.
BOY: You gonna come back? You're gonna come back?
GEOFF: I dunno.
BOY: Where's the mission?
GEOFF: Dunno!
BOY: Look 'ere… your sister's crying.
GEOFF: I know. You better go, Gary, he'll be back soon.

A WELFARE OFFICER *enters and dresses* GEOFF.

[*To the audience*] On the dirt road into the mission was a big white crucifix standing as tall as a gum tree. As they dressed me in grey clothes I could hear my sisters crying and calling out for me as they led them to their dormitory. I was shown my bunk and when the lights went out I laid quietly in the darkness until the tears welled up in my eyes and I cried for my mother and father. I cried 'til I fell asleep.

> *Normie Rowe's 'It Ain't Necessarily So' plays. In a dream state, the Pharaoh's daughter wakes* GEOFF, *who then moves to* LARGY *and hugs him, before* LARGY *exits.*

[*To the audience*] In the middle of the night my father came to visit me. I only had a few minutes to hug him and tell him I wanted to come home. When he left I tried to be brave but back under my blanket I was just a boy crying for my father. That was the last time I saw him, he died a fortnight later.

> *Back to the gee fight.*

[*To* GEORGE] I'm not finished yet. That was just a lucky punch.

GEORGE: Lucky it didn't kill you.

GEOFF: I was just getting warmed up. I'm not going 'til Kid Dynamite is laying on his back.

AUNTY: Yeah, me either!

GEORGE: You don't scare us, you troublemaker.

AUNTY: Don't call my nephew a troublemaker.

GEORGE: Kid Dynamite's gonna teach you a lesson. He'll show you how much power he can pack in one punch. Come inside, ladies and gentlemen. Come and see Kid Dynamite get rid of this troublemaker once and for all.

> *The gee fight continues.* GEOFF *gets knocked down.*

1, 2, 3, 4, 5…

> AUNTY *rings the bell. All look at* AUNTY. GEORGE *grabs the bell and goes back to the fight.*

Come on! Let's box!

> *The gee fight continues.* KID DYNAMITE *gets hit and staggers before finally hitting the deck.*

1, 2, 3, 4, 5, 6… 7… 8… 9…

> KID DYNAMITE *jumps up again to fight.*

Oh! Look at that! Nothing can stop Kid Dynamite. He hasn't even worked up a sweat. The troublemaker will have to do better than that. Holda! Holda! Holda! Holda!

GEORGE's *voice fades out.* KID DYNAMITE *changes into* DALE, *a kid at the mission. He is calling out for a cow.* GEOFF *is despondent.*

DALE: [*calling*] Go...ldie! Go...ldie! Come here, girl. Got some cabbage leaves for ya! [*To* GEOFF] Break the ice on the water trough, Geoff, so the cows can have a drink. [*Calling*] Go...ldie! Ah, here she comes. [*To* GEOFF] This is your cow, Geoff. You got to feed her and milk her every morning and evening.

GEOFF *doesn't respond.*

I'm looking after you, Geoff. You're my cousin. Believe me, being a dairy boy is the best job on the mission. Look what I got here.

DALE *holds up a jam tin.*

GEOFF: What's that for?

DALE: Warm milk and a jam tin full of cream. Haw, boy, what the priests don't know won't hurt them.

GEOFF *doesn't react.*

'Ere! See this wall. Every dairy boy that's ever been here has scratched his name in the paint.

GEOFF *looks at the wall.*

That's the first one I scratched over there. DN 57.

GEOFF: You been here for four years?

DALE *doesn't hear or answer.*

DALE: Here's a clear spot, Geoff, grab one of them nails.

GEOFF: My mum's coming for me, Dale, I'm not gonna be here for four years.

Pause.

DALE: Your mum's not coming, Geoff.

GEOFF: She's gonna take me back.

DALE: She can't. And that goes for all us kids.

GEOFF: But she loves me.

Pause.

DALE: I'm sorry, Geoff. But you just got to think of other things now. Come on, scratch your name in the paint.

A MISSION PRIEST *rings a bell.*

GEOFF: GN 61... GN 62... GN 63.

    CAROLINE *enters.*

CAROLINE: I got some good news, Geoff! We're going to the Narrogin Show on the truck.

GEOFF: I already know that.

CAROLINE: I bet you didn't know Mum sent word she's gonna be there. You can tell her you're head boy now, and about Goldie. She'll be proud of you being a dairy boy.

GEOFF: I wonder if she's still got that pretty dress.

CAROLINE: I'm gonna dress up real pretty, I got some ribbons.

    Another kid, JACKIE, *enters eating from a tin.*

GEOFF: Jackie, what you got there?

JACKIE: Quiet, Geoff.

GEOFF: Did you steal it from the pantry?

JACKIE: You're not gonna dob on me, are ya? I'm cruel hungry.

GEOFF: No, you're right. But I never saw you, okay?

    FATHER LUMEN *walks on and places his hand on* GEOFF's *shoulder.*

LUMEN: It would seem to me, Geoffrey, that you don't appreciate the responsibility that goes with being head boy. Why didn't you report the theft as soon as you knew about it?

GEOFF: Jackie was hungry, Father, and I didn't want to dob.

LUMEN: So you didn't want to dob. Well, you just dobbed yourself in for some punishment. You won't be going to the Narrogin Show tomorrow. You can stay behind 'til you learn the responsibility that goes with being a head boy.

GEOFF: [*to the audience*] After not seeing my mother for three years I burst into tears. I couldn't believe that I wasn't going to see her. The next morning I raced to the top of the hill behind the church and climbed the tallest tree. I watched as the truck travelled down the old Pingeley Road past the farm and then disappeared from sight.

    At the Narrogin Showground the voices of the MISSION PRIEST *and* BELLA *cross and overlap one another.*

PRIEST: Move to the front of the truck now, girls!

BELLA: Tell Geoffrey I love him!

PRIEST: C'mon, show's over.
BELLA: Tell him Mum's very proud.
PRIEST: C'mon, find a seat.
BELLA: Don't forget now. Don't forget now.
PRIEST: Keep your arms inside the rails.
BELLA: Tell him I love him… Don't forget.
PRIEST: Watch out for the little ones.
GEOFF: I'm a dairy boy, Mum.
BELLA: Don't forget, girls.
GEOFF: Goldie's my pet cow.
BELLA: Tell him I love him.
GEOFF: I'm head boy, as well.
BELLA: Don't forget.

The PRIEST rings the bell.

GEOFF: GN 64… GN 65… GN 66.
ACTOR 1: You are fourteen now, Geoffrey.
ACTOR 2: You've shown that you have ability and strength.
ACTOR 3: We've decided that you will make a good farm labourer.
ACTOR 1: You will no longer be expected to attend classes in mathematics.
GEOFF: [*to the audience*] After three years learning to be a farm labourer I was sent to Palatine Training Centre in Perth to learn an apprenticeship.
ACTORS: [*together*] You'll make a fine cabinet-maker, Geoffrey.
GEOFF: [*to the audience*] The only problem was you had to know mathematics. I knew I was wasting my time but I was still a ward of the state.

   GEOFF'S FRIEND *runs on.*

FRIEND: I've got it!
GEOFF: Got what?
FRIEND: The tranny. The fight will be starting soon.
GEOFF: Between Lionel Rose and Harada.
FRIEND: Come on, there's no one in the hall.

   GEOFF *and his* FRIEND *listen to the fight on the tranny. Lionel Rose wins. The boys skip around as if they had won the fight themselves.* GEOFF *sees* BELLA *and* FATHER LUMEN *approaching. He goes to his room and closes the door.*

LUMEN: Open the door, Geoffrey…
BELLA: It's me, Geoffrey, your mum.
LUMEN: Open the door, Geoffrey!
BELLA: I just want to see you.
LUMEN: Your mother is here to see you.
BELLA: You're still my boy, Geoffrey.
LUMEN: You had better leave, you're only upsetting the boy. You're wasting your time, the boy's not interested.
BELLA: You're still my boy, Geoffrey. You're my boy.
GEOFF: [*to the audience*] When Mum came to visit me, I went into shock. All the years that I had hoped we could live together as a family again had turned to anger and resentment. There was only one door separating me from my mother's arms and I wanted to open it, but I couldn't.

> BELLA *goes back to her stool,* LUMEN *becomes* GEORGE *and we're back in the boxing tent.*

AUNTY: You counted too slow, he was down for the count.
GEORGE: Oh! Another troublemaker. Just like your nephew. Now you're saying I can't count.
AUNTY: Well, you can count on this.

> AUNTY *goes to hit* GEORGE *with her handbag.* KID *and* GEOFF *drag her back to her seat.*

GEOFF: Want to fight dirty, then?
KID: I'll show you how to fight dirty.

> *Both boxers take off their gloves and approach each other.* KID DYNAMITE *goes to punch* GEOFF, *but turns into his* FRIEND *and waves a note in* GEOFF*'s face.*

FRIEND: Someone asked me to give you this.
GEOFF: Who?
FRIEND: [*smelling the note*] Hmm! Baby powder.
GEOFF: All right! All right! Give it here. You haven't read it, have you?
FRIEND: Too hot for me, brother, burn my fingers.

> *He throws the note to* GEOFF *and shakes his hand as if it's burnt.* GEOFF *smells the note then reads it to himself.*

GEOFF: [*to the audience*] I was in love. Harada was out-boxed by Lionel Rose and I was king hit by Kerry. When the priest went on holidays we snuck off to the drive-in with a friend of mine and while he kissed his girlfriend on the front seat… on the back seat me and Kerry… watched the movie. I was convinced that every love song ever written had been written for us and when Lionel Rose released his hit song there was no stopping my love for Kerry.

    GEOFF *and* KERRY *waltz to Lionel Rose's love song 'I Thank You'*.

LUMEN: Narkle! In my office! Now!

    KERRY *exits and* GEOFF *goes over to* LUMEN.

This has gone too far, my boy. I know what is going on between you and Kerry. I will not tolerate sexual relationships at Palatine.

GEOFF: Excuse me, sir, but I love her too much to have sex with her.

LUMEN: Well, in my books the two go together. I'm warning you to stay away from her…

GEOFF: You don't have to worry. I'm eighteen now and I can do what I want, so I'm leaving.

LUMEN: Leaving, huh! Where to?

GEOFF: I'll stay with my aunty.

LUMEN: And where does she live?

GEOFF: In… Goldie Road, East Perth.

LUMEN: No such road.

GEOFF: Well, it's in East Perth somewhere. [*To the audience*] I felt proud of myself standing up to that priest. For the first time in my life I was making the decisions about my future. I was calling the shots, I was my own boss. So I packed my suitcase, caught a bus into town and went to the Native Welfare Department to ask for help.

ACTOR 1: Name?

GEOFF: Geoffrey Narkle.

ACTOR 2: Where have you come from?

GEOFF: Palatine Training Centre. Look, all I want to know is if there is a hostel for Noongars I can stay at.

ACTOR 3: Why did you leave Palatine Training Centre?

GEOFF: I was accused of having sex with one of the girls, so I left.

ACTOR 1: The best thing you can do is go back to Palatine.

ACTOR 2: Apologise for your behaviour.

ACTOR 3: They'll take you back.

GEOFF: Yes, I'll do that right away. Thank you for your help.

GEOFF *speaks over the Johnny O'Keefe song 'Shout'.*

What am I doing? They don't own me! I'm eighteen! I can do what I want! I'm free! I'm free! [*Shouting*] I'm free!

NOONG *is passing by with a drink.*

NOONG: You all right there, brother?

GEOFF: [*snapping out of it*] Yer! I'm okay.

NOONG: You're a Narkle, hey? I can tell by your pretty nose.

GEOFF: Yer! I'm Geoff Narkle.

NOONG: What you hanging around here for?

GEOFF: I just left Palatine. They reckon I was up to no good with one of the girls.

NOONG: You got any money?

GEOFF: Nup.

NOONG: That's okay. I've got none either. Here, have a drink. [*Calling offstage*] Hey, you mob! Come here and meet my relation Geoff Narkle.

The PARK MOB *enter. They check him out.*

GIRL: Where you from?

GEOFF: Around Narrogin. But I was brought up on the Wandering Mission.

GIRL: So you're a good boy, eh!

NOONG: Nah! They kicked him out of Palatine for kissin' all the yorgas.

GEOFF: No I didn't!

NOONG: Only jokin'. We got a place to camp not far from here and tonight we'll have a party and you can meet the rest of the mob.

The actors dance to Johnny O'Keefe's 'Wild One' until one of them passes out. The lights fade to morning. The sound of birds.

GEOFF: [*to the audience*] My first taste of freedom included my first taste of beer [*drum beat*] and from that to Brandivino [*drum beat*] and then to plonk [*drum beat*]. I woke up on a verandah in North Perth somewhere. I'd lost my suitcase but it didn't worry me, no one else had one. From then on I spent most of my time drinking and patching up money to buy more drink. Sometimes we had a house to sleep in and sometimes we slept in the park.

NOONG *walks in with his shoulders back.*

NOONG: Hey, cuz. You won't be seeing me around the park any more.

GEOFF: You goin' to the clink.

NOONG: Aagh! Go away.

GEOFF: Where you going, then?

NOONG: I'm gonna sign up for the army. The way I figure it, it'll be just like the mission. Food, clothes, told what to do. The only difference is you get paid for it.

GEOFF: Hey, yeh! We're already trained.

NOONG *and* GEOFF *stand in a line facing a* MAN. *With his back to the audience, we only hear his voice.*

MAN'S VOICE: Next!

GEOFF: Isn't there a war on?

NOONG: I don't know.

MAN'S VOICE: Next!

GEOFF: Yeh, there's Normie Rowe, got called up.

NOONG: Don't be an idiot, he's a singer not a soldier.

MAN'S VOICE: Next!

GEOFF: Well, so was Elvis and he got called up.

NOONG: Nah! You're getting mixed up with that movie *GI Blues*.

MAN'S VOICE: Next!

GEOFF: I'm sure there is a war on. In Asia!

NOONG: You don't mean Vietnam?

GEOFF: Yeah, that's it.

NOONG: My cousin got sent there.

MAN'S VOICE: Name?

NOONG *and* GEOFF *run away.*

GEOFF: Stuff this, at least on the mission we didn't get shot at.

NOONG: Jeez, Geoffrey, that was a stupid idea, you could have got us killed.

GEOFF: Me?

NOONG: Anyway, I've got a better idea.

GEOFF: And what's that?

NOONG: George Stewart's boxing troupe is going on tour. We'll join up.

GEOFF: I can't box. I'd get killed. I might as well go to Vietnam.

NOONG: Stand up straight, let me have a look at ya.

NOONG *checks him up and down.*

The yorgas go mad for boxers.

GEOFF: That's no good if I'm all busted up.

NOONG: Ah, you got nothing to worry about, the first fight is in Narrogin, your home town. No one's gonna hurt you there.

GEOFF: Yer. That's my people.

NOONG: Hey, George!

GEORGE *enters.*

This is the fella I was talking about. Geoff Narkle meet George Stewart.

GEORGE: Where you from, boy?

GEOFF: Narrogin.

GEORGE: Nah, that's no good. Where else?

GEOFF: Albany.

GEORGE: Al... Alba... aah, that's no good either.

GEOFF: Mount Barker's close by.

GEORGE: Mount Barker, eh! That's perfect!

The scene changes to the boxing tent. A drum beat starts and a CROWD *assembles.*

There's gonna be a fight in this house! There's gonna be a fight in this house! We'll fight any man, black, white, blue or brindle! Come and see my fighters! Come and see my champions! They're the best in the land, they'll fight any man. Holda! Holda! Holda! There he is now, the Barker Bulldog. Take a good look because you'll never see him again. When you get the gloves on you won't see a thing. His left hand will never be out of your face. He'll stop ya! Block ya! And make you scream for mercy. He'll nibble you in the first round, he'll bite you in the second and chew you up and spit you out in the third.

The drum stops. Everyone but GEOFF *freezes.*

GEOFF: [*to the audience*] As I stood on the planks, supported by forty-four gallon drums, my legs were shaking so much I thought I was going to faint and fall headfirst into the crowd, but as George did his spruiking I was comforted by the thought that this was my home town.

The drum.

GEORGE: Do we have any takers for the boy who's come back to fight in his home town?! Holda! Holda! Holda! My goodness! There's gonna be a fight in this house. I've never seen so many fighters in the one town. One at a time, one at a time, you'll all get a chance to fight the Barker Bulldog.

Everyone but GEOFF *freezes.*

GEOFF: [*to the audience*] People or not, they all reckoned by the way my legs were shaking they had a good chance of beating me. And no one likes a big shot, especially from your home town.

GEOFF *and the other boxer,* CHARLIE, *warm up on the ropes.* AUNTY *approaches the tent.*

GEORGE: No! Ladies aren't allowed to fight in the tent.
AUNTY: But I reckon I can beat him.
GIRL: Me too!
CHARLIE: Barker Bulldog, huh! I'll make you jump, Narkle.
GEOFF: Hey? You're my cousin Charlie.

GEOFF *goes to shake hands with* CHARLIE. CHARLIE *hits* GEOFF's *hand then the back of his head.* GEOFF *runs out of the ring.*

GEORGE: Get back in the ring, Geoff.
GEOFF: Nah, George, he hit me.
GEORGE: You're a tent boxer now. I'll take care of the fight! Get back into the ring!

GEORGE *pulls* GEOFF *through the ropes back into the ring.*

CHARLIE: Lay down and let me win the money.
GEOFF: I can't do that!
CHARLIE: You're my cousin, aren't ya?
GEOFF: Yer, but…

GEOFF *gets punched again.*

You're my cousin, hey Charlie?
CHARLIE: Yeah!
GEOFF: We look after one another, hey Charlie?
CHARLIE: Yeah!
GEOFF: You want me to lay down?
CHARLIE: Yep!
GEOFF: Well, you go first.

> GEOFF *king hits* CHARLIE *and knocks him out.*

GEORGE: Aagh! You'll have to do better than that! Who's next? Who's next? Who's gonna fight the Barker Bulldog?

GEOFF: [*to the audience*] By the end of the day I'd had five fights. Won one, drew one and lost the next three. In the morning as we pulled the tent down I felt like a hero. I was the boxer with the best name and the sorest nose in the south-west. I got three square meals a day, polony, dry bread and Coke. After a few more towns I started to win a few fights. It was a hard life for a tent boxer but it was a way of earning respect.

> *Normie Rowe's 'Shakin' All Over' has the* GIRL *swoon. The boxers shake hands with* GEORGE *who gives them their money. At the end of the music* GEOFF *starts shadowboxing.*

GEORGE: He'll make a good partner; this is his third year in the troupe.

KID: You reckon he's got it in him?

GEORGE: Only one way to find out. Hey, Bulldog! I want to pull you out of fake fighting for a while.

GEOFF: What do you want to do that for? I've been winning, George.

GEORGE: Come here. I want you to insult Dynamite for me.

GEOFF: I can't do that, he's my cobber.

GEORGE: Nah, it's just for fun, Geoff.

GEOFF: All right… You idiot.

GEORGE: Nah, that's no good. C'mon, beef it up a little.

GEOFF: You couldn't fight your way out of a wet paper bag.

GEORGE: That's better! Keep going.

GEOFF: Where'd you get your pretty belt buckle from, your girlfriend?

KID: Hey, you leave my girlfriend out of this.

> KID *shirtfronts* GEOFF.

GEORGE: Settle down, boys. I want you to gee fight with Kid Dynamite. You do as I say and you can box and keep your pretty nose as well.

GEOFF: Yeah! Yeah! Yeah!

KID: Yeah! Yeah! Yeah!

GEORGE: Come inside, ladies and gentlemen, now we've got a real fight on our hands.

> KID *and* GEOFF *fight bare-handed.* KID *has* GEOFF *on the ground, throttling him, when* AUNTY *runs in, hitting* KID *with her bag.*

AUNTY: You're not going to hurt my nephew, you bastard!
GEOFF: It's all right, Aunty, I'm okay! It's a fake fight!
KID: Get her off me, Geoff! She's got a brick in her bag!
GEOFF: You all right, Dynamite?

> GEORGE *wrestles* AUNTY *to the corner.*

GEORGE: Next time, Geoff, keep your aunty out of the tent. Come on! On the truck, Royal Show tomorrow.
GEOFF: [*to the audience*] After four years I was still on the back of a truck going from one agricultural show to the next. Being a boxer didn't mean anything to me any more. On the outside I was the Barker Bulldog but on the inside I was still the boy back on the mission having nightmares every time I fell asleep. [*To* GEORGE] Stop the truck, George!

> GEORGE *walks away from the truck and towards* GEOFF.

GEORGE: It's only a rusty T-Model, Geoff, get back in the truck.
GEOFF: It's a Cadillac, George, Blackfellas' Cadillac.
GEORGE: Come on, Bulldog, gotta set up for the Royal Show tomorrow.
GEOFF: I'm not going, George… Catch ya later, Dynamite.

> GEOFF *hitchhikes to Normie Rowe's 'Que Sera'. He enters* BELLA*'s camp.*

BELLA: I knew you were coming. It's been a long time, Geoff.
GEOFF: I want to stay here, Mum… with you.
BELLA: Here?
GEOFF: We need to talk, Mum.
BELLA: There's nothin' to talk about.
GEOFF: Well, why…?

> BELLA *turns her back, pauses, then faces* GEOFF.

BELLA: You don't belong here, Geoffrey.
GEOFF: Well, where do I belong?
BELLA: Not here!
GEOFF: We got to talk, Mum. We gotta talk.

> *A drum beat.* GEORGE *is spruiking again.*

GEORGE: Do we have any takers?! We'll fight any man, black, white, blue or brindle! Do we have any takers?! Come inside, come inside, bring your wife, bring someone else's wife, it's all the same to me!

There's gonna be a fight in this house! There's gonna be a fight in this house! Holda! Holda! Holda! Oh, I see the Barker Bulldog's returned after all the work's been done.

GEOFF: I want to fight, George.

GEORGE: I got someone to replace you, Bulldog.

GEOFF: I don't want to fight for you, George, I just want to fight.

GEORGE looks at the YOUNG BOXER.

GEORGE: Okay, Bulldog, just one fight.

GEOFF: [*to the audience*] As I looked at my replacement it was like staring at myself four years before at the Narrogin Show. A young Noongar boy not fighting for the money or the sport, but as a way of earning respect. When the first round started I saw fear in his eyes as he saw a lifetime of anger in mine.

GEOFF begins shadowboxing, facing the audience. The CROWD barracks for him, then taunts him.

ACTOR 1: Your sisters are crying.

ACTOR 2: Open the door, Geoffrey!

ACTOR 3: You gonna come back?

ACTORS: [*together*] You gonna come back?

The three actors repeat these lines three times as they move to the corners of the ring with their backs to GEOFF. The song 'Pick Me Up' is playing. GEOFF wanders around to each actor looking for a friend. Their backs remain turned away.

GEOFF: [*to the audience*] Hotels and parks became my boxing tent, and an abandoned house opposite Fremantle Prison became my home. Every morning I gave the tower guards an early morning call. [*To the guards*] Up yours, ya dogs! Come down here and fight!

NOONG enters and tries to pull GEOFF back.

NOONG: Give it a rest, Geoffrey. You've been doing it every morning for a fortnight.

GEOFF: Come down out of your tower and have a go, ya dogs!

NOONG: Geoffrey, they got guns!

GEOFF: And bring ya guns with ya! You don't scare me!

NOONG: You kartwarra, Geoffrey! You're gonna get us in big trouble!

GEOFF: You tell them boys in there Geoff Narkle says hello, and I'll see you tomorrow!

NOONG: Here, have a drink, it'll settle ya down.

> GEOFF *pushes* NOONG *away as a* WHITE MAN *walks past.*

GEOFF: What are you staring at?

MAN: Aah! I wasn't staring at anything.

GEOFF: Take a good look!

MAN: I don't want any trouble, okay!

GEOFF: You never seen an Abo before, nigger, boong. Have a good look. Come on, have a good look! You can't help yourself, can ya?! You're just like those bastards in the tower.

MAN: Hey, look! I don't want any trouble, okay?

> GEOFF *forces the* MAN *backwards along the path and starts chipping him. Drumbeats in the background.*

GEOFF: [*to the audience*] After nearly killing a man I realised I'd forgotten who I was and where I'd come. I had to talk to Mum about what was eating me up inside so I headed back to Mount Barker to try and talk to her again.

> BELLA *enters.*

[*To* BELLA] You remember that old dog Two-Up, Mum, when he used to run around that stump?

BELLA: You remember that? They were the good old days.

GEOFF: You know, one time when I was travelling with the boxing troupe I saw Dad's old T-Model rusting away near Fowlers. Huh, Blackfellas' Cadillac.

BELLA: You want a cup of tea, Geoff?

GEOFF: He came to visit me one night at the mission before he passed away.

BELLA: I'll put the billy on.

GEOFF: He told me he loved me and told me not to cry. But I did, Mum, I cried. I cried for you too.

BELLA: We can't change what happened, Geoff.

GEOFF: But we can talk about it.

> *A big pause.* BELLA *looks back at* GEOFF.

BELLA: I cried too. It killed me inside when they took you kids away. [*She walks to the front of the stage.*] When me and your father got back all I could see was your footprints in the sand and the knucklebones where you'd been playing. That's all I had left… that's all I had left.

BELLA *and* GEOFF *hug, then* BELLA *goes back to her seat.*

GEOFF: [*to the audience*] Just before Mum passed away we were able to talk about what had happened to myself and my sisters. We cried more than we talked. As the cockatoos disappeared into the gum trees I think of old man Abram and all the old Noongars who spent their last days fenced in by a rubbish tip, a farmer's barbed-wire fence and a big white sign. From up on the Granite Ridge, as I look towards the town of Narrogin, a cold wind blows through the scrub that was once Clayton Road Reserve.

THE END

GLOSSARY

caarda	goanna
manatj	police
Noongars	Aboriginal people of south-west Australia
rat ban	police van
wadjulla	white people
yorgas	women

Rainbow's End

Jane Harrison

Jane Harrison, a Muruwari descendant, was commissioned by Ilbijerri Theatre Co-operative to write *Stolen*, about the Stolen Generations. *Stolen* premiered in 1998, followed by seven annual seasons in Melbourne, plus tours to Sydney, Adelaide, regional Victoria, Tasmania, the UK (twice), Hong Kong and Tokyo, and readings in Canada and New York. Jane was the co-winner (with Dallas Winmar for *Aliwa!*) of the Kate Challis RAKA Award for *Stolen*. *Stolen* is studied on the VCE English and NSW HSC syllabi. *On a Park Bench* was workshopped at Playbox and the Banff Playrites Colony, and was a finalist in the Lake Macquarie Drama Prize. *Rainbow's End* premiered in 2005 at the Melbourne Museum and toured to Mooroopna, and then to Japan in 2007. Jane was the 2006 Theatrelab Indigenous Award winner for her most recent play, *Blakvelvet*. She contributed one chapter to *Many Voices, Reflections on experiences of Indigenous child separation*, published by the National Library, Canberra. Her greatest creations are her two daughters.

From left: Pauline Whyman as Gladys, Beryl Booth as Nan Dear and Tammy Clarkson as Dolly in the Ilbijerri Theatre Co-operative production of RAINBOW'S END, 2005. (Photo: Cathryn Tremain, The Age Photo Sales)

FIRST PERFORMANCE

Rainbow's End was first produced by Ilbijerri Theatre Co-operative at Bunjilaka, the Aboriginal Centre at Melbourne Museum, on 18 February 2005, with the following cast:

NAN DEAR	Beryl Booth
GLADYS	Pauline Whyman
DOLLY	Tammy Clarkson
ERROL FISHER	Gareth Ellis

Director, Wesley Enoch
Designer, Christina Smith
Lighting Designer, Marko Respondeck
Sound Designer, David Franzke

ACKNOWLEDGEMENT

The author and publisher gratefully acknowledge permission to quote from 'Que Sera, Sera', words and music by Ray Evans and Jay Livingston. © St Angelo Music adm. by Universal Music Publishing Pty Ltd. © Jay Livingston Music. For Australia and New Zealand: Alfred Publishing (Australia) Pty Ltd (ABN 15 003 954 247), PO Box 2355, Taren Point, NSW 2229. International copyright secured. All rights reserved. Unauthorised reproduction is illegal. Reprinted with permission.

AUTHOR'S NOTE

Rainbow's End was commissioned by Ilbijerri Aboriginal and Torres Strait Islander Theatre Co-operative. The original brief was to tell a decade of Victorian Koori history and to write about 'the heroes'. There were many heroes in that era, but I was drawn to the 'unsung' heroes, and in particular the women who fought the good fight in their daily struggles to keep their families together, house, feed, cloth, educate and, above all, love and protect their children. (And aren't we all still fighting that good fight?) It's always a bittersweet experience researching the kinds of plays I'm drawn to write. Perhaps not bitter—a deep sadness for what our Elders had to suffer due to their Aboriginal heritage, sweet because of the poignant stories many of the Elders shared with me. Some of the Aunties that I spoke to recalled the freedom that they felt as children living on The Flats—that area between Shepparton and Mooroopna where many Aboriginal families lived on the fringe. They remember being protected from the reality of their often dire circumstances by their Elders—that was 'grown-up business'.

I want to emphasise that *Rainbow's End* is a work of fiction—the characters and personal interactions portrayed are not based on real people or events, but I do hope they have an emotional truth. The exception are those historical events which provide a backdrop to the play, such as the Queen's visit and the development of the Rumbalara housing which occurred during the 1950s. I would like to express my sincere admiration to those families who lived on The Flats, and those who endured similar challenges, with thanks to all those who shared their stories. Thanks also to Ilbijerri and the fabulous and dedicated director, cast and crew who brought the story to life in its first production.

Jane Harrison

CHARACTERS

Family on The Flats:

NAN DEAR, matriarch of the family, sixties
GLADYS BANKS, Nan's daughter, Dolly's mother, forties
DOLLY BANKS, Gladys's daughter, seventeen/eighteen
ERROL FISHER, whitefella, twentyish

Other characters, to be played by the actor playing Errol:

BANK MANAGER
INSPECTOR
MR COODY, the rent collector
JUNGI, policeman
PAPA DEAR

VARIOUS OFFSTAGE VOICES (COUSIN, CROWD, COUNCILLORS, RADIO ANNOUNCERS, PRESENTERS)

SETTING

1950s. A humpy on the riverbank. Clean and homely.

Also: Daisch's Paddock (town tip); cork trees; bank manager's office; dance hall; new Rumbalara housing; and town hall.

ACT ONE

PROLOGUE: AFTERMATH

The song 'Que Sera, Sera' is heard:

> *Que sera, sera*
> *Whatever will be, will be,*
> *The future's not ours to see*
> *Que sera, sera.*

It's late spring, late afternoon and gloomy outside. Inside their humpy NAN DEAR *and* GLADYS *are rebuilding after a flood has devastated their home. Everything below three feet is sodden and mud-splattered.* GLADYS *mops, wrings out and removes things that are destroyed.* NAN *finishes hanging a piece of hessian to replace a ruined piece that lined the interior walls. Now she covers the hessian with pages from a magazine.*

NAN DEAR: [*pointing to some magazines*] Pass those.
GLADYS: They're Dolly's.
NAN DEAR: They're dry.

> GLADYS *hands them over.* NAN *rips the pages, slowly and deliberately, pastes them with homemade glue and sticks them, upside down, onto the hessian.*
>
> *After a time* DOLLY *arrives home from school and surveys the scene critically. She toes the old, ruined lino. She sighs, resigned. Until she spots her magazines. She goes to protest but sighs again, resigned.* GLADYS *fakes cheerfulness.*

GLADYS: It'll be all right.
DOLLY: You always say that.

> NAN *and* GLADYS *take a quick look at each other.* NAN *gestures for* DOLLY *to come over. She does and* NAN *gives her granddaughter a hug.*
>
> *The lights go down.*

◆◆◆◆◆

SCENE ONE (A): THE QUEEN'S VISIT

Humpy interior. Morning. GLADYS *is getting dressed up and humming to herself.* DOLLY *has her head down over her schoolbooks.*

GLADYS *listens in rapt silence to the voice of Queen Elizabeth II on the radio.*

RADIO: [*voice-over*] … standing at last on Australian soil, on this spot, which is the birthplace of the nation, I want to tell you all, how happy I am to be amongst you, and how much I look forward to my journey amongst Australia…

The radio fades out as NAN *enters.*

GLADYS: That valve… Where's my white gloves?

NAN DEAR: Gloves? Don't need white gloves to pick beans.

GLADYS *doesn't react.*

You're going into town then, for all that hullabaloo. Think of inviting me?

GLADYS: You? I know how you feel about royalty. Even if she is the 'first reigning monarch to visit our shores'.

DOLLY: Nan, I need your help with this.

She is doing homework.

NAN DEAR: One loyal subject in the family is enough. And someone's got to pick.

DOLLY: I'm doing our family tree.

NAN DEAR: Tree?

GLADYS: Don't know about loyal. Just going for a squiz.

NAN DEAR: Don't know where you get these ideas from sometimes.

GLADYS: I'm not hurting anyone, am I? It's a moment I'll remember… to see our pretty young monarch and the Duke. I'm not going to miss it for all the tea in China!

GLADYS *flounces out to the back room.*

DOLLY: Nan?

NAN DEAR: [*to herself*] Tree? [*To* DOLLY] You mean the biyala? Spirit tree, branches hanging low over the river?

DOLLY: Like this.

NAN *looks over* DOLLY'*s shoulder to see the diagram she is making.*

I need to list all our family members... our parents and their parents and so on...

> NAN *picks up a pencil and begins to write over* DOLLY'*s shoulder.*

...but not cousins.

> NAN *stops writing.*

NAN DEAR: And why not cousins? What kind of a fool thing...? You need to know who your cousins are. So you don't marry 'em.

> GLADYS *returns.*

GLADYS: Queen Victoria married her cousin—'Prince Albert of Saxe-Coburg'.

NAN DEAR: Well, we don't.

DOLLY: [*baiting her*] And Mum told me that 'our lovely young monarch', married her Greek/German cousin, Prince Philip—

GLADYS: My glory, it was a beautiful wedding—

NAN DEAR: Hmmp. No good'll come of it. Their children will be retarded, or, or worse, funny in the head.

> *Beat.*

GLADYS: Could you listen out for the taxi?

NAN DEAR: [*incredulous*] The taxi?

GLADYS: It's Aunty's shoes. I don't want Her Majesty to see them dirty.

> NAN *just shakes her head in disgust.* DOLLY *giggles, then stops as* NAN *glares at her.* GLADYS *gets money out of the jam tins for the taxi.*

DOLLY: I gotta put down where you were born, Nan.

NAN DEAR: My birth certificate says 'Murray River'. Born there and, by crikey, I'm gunna go back and die there.

DOLLY: Nan, you're not gunna die. You're gunna live forever.

NAN DEAR: Well, of course I'm not gunna die. Not here, anyway. Gotta go back to me old place to do that. And I'll have a feed of—

DOLLY: Swan eggs.

NAN DEAR: [*threatening*] Deary me, that girl mustn't want help with her homework...

> DOLLY *looks contrite.*

Swan eggs, before I go.

DOLLY: [*to herself*] Mother, Gladys Banks. Grandmother, Alice Louise Cooper. Nan, if you love that Murray River so much, why don't you still live there?
NAN DEAR: [*bitter, half to herself*] They forced us to leave. Forced us to leave Cummeragunja. Our home.
DOLLY: Who, Nan? Who did?

> *But* NAN *doesn't want to talk about that business and* DOLLY *knows it. She goes back to her homework.*

Grandmother, Alice Cooper who married Reginald Harold Dear. Reginald Harold Dear's parents are... Nan?
NAN DEAR: Is that your taxi, Gladys? [*Cagily*] I don't keep details like that in me head.
DOLLY: [*to herself*] You do so.

> GLADYS *rushes over to the window.*

My great grandparents, Nan...
GLADYS: No...
DOLLY: Nan?
NAN DEAR: [*to* GLADYS] You'd better wait on the track. Else the taxi will pick up one of the cork-tree lads. [*Dryly*] I'm sure they'll want to celebrate the Queen's visit.
GLADYS: Oo, I hadn't thought of that... How do I look?
DOLLY: Fit for a queen!

> GLADYS *is pleased by the compliment but pretends not to show it.*
>
> *The lights change to a dream sequence:* GLADYS, *curtsying, is presenting a bouquet of flowers to the* QUEEN. *Instead of being formal, the* QUEEN *pulls her into a hug.*
>
> *The lights come back to reality.* GLADYS *is holding a bunch of weeds. She looks at them as if she can't understand why she is holding them. She waves goodbye and leaves.*

[*Dismayed*] So it's buka bung stew tonight!
NAN DEAR: If I don't get on that truck and do an honest day's work, it will be. And you, off to school.
DOLLY: But I haven't finished—
NAN DEAR: Quick... go. But keep away from them cork trees.
DOLLY: Yes, Nan. You've told me a hundred times.

NAN DEAR: Don't be cheeky.
DOLLY: Yes, Nan.
NAN DEAR: Good girl.
DOLLY: Yes, Nan.

> DOLLY *exits.*
> *The lights indicate a time change.*

♦♦♦♦♦

SCENE ONE (B)

The radio is heard featuring a description of the Queen's 1954 Royal Tour of Australia.

ANNOUNCER: [*voice-over*] In every town it was something different. In Shepparton, it was babies. My word, babies everywhere! All washed and dress and fit to meet the band. No wonder the Duke called out, 'Where's Father?'

> GLADYS, *holding a very wilted bunch of flowers, comes inside the humpy and plonks down in the only chair. She kicks off her shoes.* DOLLY *watches her.* NAN *is cooking.*

GLADYS: Oh, my feet! Remind me never to borrow Aunty's shoes again.
NAN DEAR: What about the taxi?
GLADYS: Didn't show, did it? So I walked up to the causeway—
NAN DEAR: That's not far.
GLADYS: Then all the way to Shepp.
NAN DEAR: To Shepp? Why?
GLADYS: On account of the hessian.
NAN DEAR: What hessian?
GLADYS: The hessian they lined the road with. The hessian that I couldn't get through and couldn't even peek over.
DOLLY: What they do that for?
GLADYS: Stop the likes of her seeing our humpies.
NAN DEAR: Dolly, bring the wood in.

> DOLLY *sighs and exits.*

GLADYS: If they'd given us better houses… But hessian! Like a band-aid over a sore—

NAN DEAR: What are they going to do with all that hessian?

GLADYS: Oh, Mum, doesn't it bother you?

NAN DEAR: What good is it if I get het up? My job is to get food on the table—

GLADYS: But decent housing, Mum—

NAN DEAR: Gladys, get off your high horse. Least here we do things our way—no one breathin' down our necks. Not like those last days at Cummeragunja. [*Beat.*] Anyway, it's Papa Dear's mission to make things better for the Aboriginal people. [*Beat.*] Papa Dear had a meetin' with her, you know.

GLADYS: Our head of state? He had a meeting? With our queen?

NAN DEAR: She's not my queen. But yes, that's how important—

GLADYS: —he is.

NAN DEAR: —she is—getting a meeting with the busiest Aboriginal around!

GLADYS: Why didn't you tell me?

NAN DEAR: I just did. He popped in to see us. But you were out gallivanting.

GLADYS: I missed him…? Did he say what she was like?

NAN DEAR: For goodness' sake!

    DOLLY *returns and is listening with interest.*

GLADYS: And I was just hoping for a glimpse.

DOLLY: Did you get one?

GLADYS: No…

NAN DEAR: Gawd, daught, where do you get these highfalutin ideas from?

GLADYS: Well, it's either from you, or it's from Papa Dear, and somehow I don't think it's from—

NAN DEAR: Don't just sit there, girl. Stoke the fire.

DOLLY: Yes, Nan.

GLADYS: Yes, Mum.

    The radio fades up again.

ANNOUNCER: [*voice-over*] And just to remind the royal couple that they were in Australia, we showed them how to throw a boomerang… It really does come back…

    The lights go down.

◆◆◆◆◆

SCENE TWO (A): OH, ERROL

As the lights come up, GLADYS *is chopping wood with an axe and listening to Bob Dyer's quiz show,* Pick-A-Box, *on the radio.*

BOB DYER: [*radio voice-over*] With what is the tail of the beaver covered?

GLADYS: [*to herself*] The answer to that'd be scales.

CONTESTANT: [*radio voice-over*] Fur?

She pauses, waiting for the answer.

BOB DYER: [*radio voice-over*] I'm sorry, it's scales! An unusual bit of nature there.

GLADYS: 'Course.

She resumes chopping.

BOB DYER: [*radio voice-over*] What is the more common term for an ocular contusion?

NAN *appears, carrying two dead rabbits.*

GLADYS: A black eye.

NAN DEAR: Whose black eye? You mean, Ester's—

GLADYS: Shh!

NAN DEAR: [*to herself*] Oh, that. [*Giving the radio a dirty look*] Thought you were talkin' sense for once.

NAN *starts to skin the rabbits.*

CONTESTANT: [*radio voice-over*] A swollen eye? A damaged eye?

Pause.

BOB DYER: [*radio voice-over*] Yes! That's good enough! I was debating that for a moment! You were quite correct, medically. But, to put it bluntly, the more down-to-earth one is…

GLADYS & BOB DYER: [*simultaneously*] … a black eye.

DOLLY *steps outside the humpy, throws out the tea leaves from the billy, and pauses. She is chewing gum.*

DOLLY: Who's got a black eye?

NAN DEAR: Doesn't concern you, Dolly.

NAN *turns the station on the radio.* GLADYS *goes back to her chopping.*

DOLLY: You should go on *Pick-A-Box*, Mum, you're ace.
NAN DEAR: A black contestant? I'd like to see that!
DOLLY: How could they tell?

> *She has a sly look at* NAN, *then flicks the radio back to* Pick-A-Box.

BOB DYER: [*radio voice-over*] Our next contestant is petite and lovely. Who is she?

> *A female voice on the radio is heard giggling.*
>
> NAN *looks at* DOLLY *who turns the radio off.*

DOLLY: [*dreamily*] One of the boxes has a real mink stole, from the House of Biba. I could see you picking up that prize, eh, Mum?
NAN DEAR: A mink stole around here?
GLADYS: And why not, Mum? It gets cold at night here, too.
NAN DEAR: Just not going to happen. Not in my lifetime.
DOLLY: I bet there's a lot of things that you couldn't have imagined, Nan. Bodgies and widgies, canned food—
NAN DEAR: That's been around. Saved our skins many a time.
DOLLY: —the hokey-pokey… [*She dances around.*] I'll teach you, Nan.
NAN DEAR: Can't teach an old dog new tricks.
DOLLY: [*dreamily*] Maybe Mum will surprise you…

> *The lights change for a dream sequence.*
>
> *The radio crackles to life.*

BOB DYER: [*radio voice-over*] Howdy, customers. We're in the third week of our Melbourne season…
DOLLY DYER: [*radio voice-over*] And our latest contestant is Mrs Gladys Banks from Moo—roo—
GLADYS: That's Mooroopna.
BOB DYER: [*radio voice-over*] Just to recap…You won two prizes, didn't you? A sewing machine that does everything under the sun—overlocking, buttonholes, embroidery stitches—and a mink stole!
DOLLY DYER: [*radio voice-over*] From the House of Biba, Gladys…

> *The scene fades out as the lights fade back to reality.*

DOLLY: Mum'll be on the radio, she'll win all those wonderful prizes, she'll be a hero—

GLADYS: [*correcting her*] Heroine.
NAN DEAR: Why you don't listen to Jack Davey, Gladys. At least he's Australian, not one of them flash Yanks.
DOLLY: Get with the times, Nan, this is the fifties!

> NAN *turns her full attention to* DOLLY.

NAN DEAR: I've heard you were talking to Leon Arnold.
DOLLY: So?
NAN DEAR [*threatening her*] Speak cheek to me... Where were you talking?
DOLLY: Just... along the track...
NAN DEAR: He's your uncle's cousin.
DOLLY : I'm not marrying the boy. [*Learned by rote*] After all, I can't marry an Arnold, can't marry an Anderson, can't marry a Brock.
GLADYS: You can't marry anyone—
DOLLY: —they're all related—
GLADYS: —least not till you've finished your studies. And get a good job. In town—
DOLLY: By then I'll be old. How old were you, Nan?

> *Her chewing-gum bubble pops.*

NAN DEAR: Just get the water.
DOLLY: Yes, Nan.
NAN DEAR: And don't let that boy get fresh. He's got a wild look.
DOLLY: No, Nan.
NAN DEAR: [*to herself*] Motherless child, poor lad...
GLADYS: And practise your French verbs.
DOLLY: Oui, Madame.
NAN DEAR & GLADYS: [*simultaneously*] Good girl!

> DOLLY *pushes an old pram, which holds a kero tin, in the direction of the river. They watch her depart, then both sigh.*

NAN DEAR: French verbs! Mink stoles! You put ideas into that girl's head.
GLADYS: She needs to know the world is bigger than just this.
NAN DEAR: She doesn't need to know any more than she does. [*Beat. Holding up a rabbit*] I'm taking this over to Ester's. Seems they're in a bit of a spot. She's with child again...
GLADYS: Oh, I didn't know—

NAN DEAR: … and she woke up with an [*mimicking* BOB DYER] ocular contusion… from that whitefella husband of hers.

GLADYS: I hadn't heard.

NAN DEAR: If you spent less time on them quiz shows, you'd know more.

GLADYS: Yes, Mum.

NAN exits with rabbit in hand.

♦ ♦ ♦ ♦ ♦

SCENE TWO (B)

The lights come up on DOLLY *pushing the pram, while a Brylcreemed lad,* ERROL, *wobbles up on a bicycle from the opposite direction. He nearly falls off his bike at the sight of her.*

ERROL: Morning, miss.

DOLLY nods and ERROL checks out the contents of the pram as he passes. Once they have passed each other they look back and check each other out—an instant spark of attraction passing between them. DOLLY *exits.*

ERROL *dismounts and studies his map. He looks puzzled, but puts the map away and pushes on towards* GLADYS, *who is still chopping wood.*

ERROL *pulls out a heavy book from the pannier on his bike and takes a tentative step towards* GLADYS.

Excuse me, sir…

She stands there with the axe.

GLADYS: Yes? Can I help you, lad?

ERROL: Sorry, er, ma'am. [*Extremely nervous*] My name is Errol Fisher. I am a representative of… er… I am in this area today, with quite an amazing offer. Um… I have a presentation regarding…

He offers the book. GLADYS *looks at it with interest.*

As you can see… it is that most famous of tomes, the—

DOLLY *has returned and at the sight of her* ERROL *clumsily drops the book.* GLADYS *picks it up…*

DOLLY: I don't think so, mister. They're not for the likes of us.

... and dusts it off tenderly. She hands it back to him.

ERROL: [*defeated*] : Rightio.

ERROL turns his bike around.

GLADYS: Wait. [*To* DOLLY] Haven't you got a job to do?

ERROL turns back, a glimmer of hope. DOLLY *puts her nose in the air and exits.*

[*To* ERROL] What did you say that was?

ERROL: It is…

Celestial music is heard for a moment.

… the Encyclopedia Britannica! If I could be permitted to demonstrate its points, its, um, say… say…

GLADYS: Salient?

ERROL: Yes, salient points… Rather, if I could just—at least—run through my, you know… Well, I would truly appreciate it—

GLADYS: Sit down, son.

ERROL notices GLADYS *is sitting on a kero tin so he does the same.*

ERROL: Presenting… the Encyclopedia Britannica. [*His spiel begins.*] Your entrée to the world of learning, a world of discovery, a world of fascinating facts…

GLADYS *flicks through the book with interest.*

GLADYS: Like on *Pick-A-Box*?

ERROL: Yes! One of last year's contestants read the Britannica for half an hour each night, and attributed that to the secret of his, his, um…

GLADYS: Success?

ERROL: Yes! His success!

GLADYS: Only half an hour?

ERROL: But that's not the end of it! Madam, do you have children?

GLADYS: Yeah, four of 'em. All grown up and working, except Dolly, she's my youngest. You know, Bob Dyer's wife's name is Dolly. You saw her just then—my Dolly, not Bob Dyer's Dolly.

ERROL: That was your daughter? And you're her…

GLADYS: Yes. [*With pride*] Her mother. Mrs Banks.

ERROL: Mrs Banks. [*Beat.*] Where were we? Yes—for keen fans of *Pick-A-Box*, there's nothing like the Britannica... er... Children—you have four... um...

GLADYS: But only one at home, the boys are all away shearing.

ERROL: Yes... because it is for school-aged children... [*Nodding in* DOLLY's *direction*] She's...?

GLADYS: School-aged. Nearly seventeen.

ERROL: Ah! ... that this encyclopedia set is most beneficial. It will open up a world of dis...

GLADYS: Discovery.

ERROL: Discovery... set them up on a lifelong love of learning, help with school assignments, allowing them to reach their full potential...

The lights change for a dream sequence. GLADYS *sees* DOLLY *in a robe and clapboard hat.*

GLADYS: [*to herself*] My girl, a graduate...

The lighting fades back to reality. GLADYS *looks around, fearful that her 'daydream' has been witnessed, but it hasn't.* NAN *returns.* ERROL *rises politely.*

ERROL: Ma'am.

NAN DEAR: [*hissing to* GLADYS, *jutting her lips in* ERROL's *direction*] What's he doing here? He's not the Welfare?

GLADYS: No.

NAN DEAR: Churchy type? Tell him we only got time for Papa Dear. He's our pastor.

GLADYS: The lad's doing a presentation.

NAN DEAR: A what?

GLADYS: Mum.

And she's dismissed. Glowering, NAN *tends the fire.*

You were saying? Set them up? Just one book will do all that?

ERROL: Not one, ma'am. Twenty-four!

GLADYS: [*faintly*] Twenty-four?

ERROL: You've seen the condensed version. Now imagine your own leather-bound library in the environment of your own home...

They are lost in their thoughts.

GLADYS: Set them up for life, you reckon?

ERROL: Er, it appears that at this point in time, I am expected to... Well, it's here that I get out the sales order form...

NAN *hovers.*

NAN DEAR: [*to* GLADYS] Ask him what it says in that there encyclops about the Aborigines, eh?

GLADYS: Now, Mum.

> ERROL *timidly flicks through the volume.*

ERROL: Er… um… it says, that… Well, I'm quite sure there's a full and very enlightening entry in the complete set.

NAN DEAR: [*to* GLADYS] Is he just?

GLADYS: Mum!

ERROL: So, Mrs, er… Banks… if you're interested, we can fill in your details…

> *He hands a fountain pen and the order form over to* GLADYS. *She freezes momentarily.* DOLLY *returns unnoticed.*

GLADYS: Now where have I placed my glasses…?

> NAN *springs into action.*

NAN DEAR: Neglected to tell you, love, I stood on 'em. Earlier. All smashed.

ERROL: That's terrible!

> DOLLY *stands over* ERROL.

DOLLY: You made a wrong turn somewhere. Hand over your map.

ERROL: [*worried*] It's the company's! If I misplace it they will dock my pay tuppence.

DOLLY: You got an encyclopedia, so how come you know nothing, eh?

ERROL: Er…

DOLLY: As Nan would say, you really came down with the last shower, didn't you? Hand it over.

ERROL: Yes, miss.

DOLLY: Here's where you went wrong. You turned onto this track, whereas you should have headed over this way and not crossed over the railway line. Here's where all the toffs live. The whitefellas in their fancy new homes that Mum reckons they think is too good for blackfellas. Shoulda known when you come across blackfella housing that you'd missed your turn-off. You must have a lousy sense of direction.

ERROL: Yes, miss.

> GLADYS *stands up and picks up the axe.*

GLADYS: Yes, son, you'd better ride on over there. That's where you'll be selling your encyclopedias. Not here.

> *The other two nod in agreement.*

ERROL: Yes, ma'am. I'll just leave my calling card. I'll write my name on it. Just in case, ma'am.

GLADYS: Don't get called that too often—ma'am. [*She laughs.*] Just in case!

ERROL: Yes, ma'am. Thank you, ma'am.

GLADYS: Dolly, show the young man the track. Point him in the right direction.

> DOLLY *and* ERROL *move off.* NAN *rushes over to* GLADYS.

NAN DEAR: [*hissing*] Call her back. Right now.

GLADYS: He's an [*with awe*] encyclopedia representative, Mum.

NAN DEAR: Think I don't know a snake-oil salesman when I see one!

GLADYS: He seems nice. Real polite. And she needs to talk to people who are doing something with their lives. People with important jobs, not just picking, like us.

NAN DEAR: We only pick 'cos that's all they'll let us do.

GLADYS: Exactly.

> NAN *is watching* DOLLY *and* ERROL *suspiciously from the window.*

NAN DEAR: Anyway, he smells of perfume. What kind of fella smells of perfume?

> GLADYS *starts singing 'I've Got the World on a String'. She is looking at Errol's card.* NAN *notices.*

Now, Gladys, you won't be needing any of them encyclops. Won't help you answer any more questions on the *Colgate Palmolive Pick-A-Box*, will it?

GLADYS: Yes, Mum. No, Mum.

NAN DEAR: That's right! So don't go getting ideas. Hardly got two pennies to rub together.

> GLADYS *continues to sing softly, as the spotlight goes on* DOLLY *and* ERROL.

DOLLY: Sold many?
ERROL: Um… This is my first presentation. Well, the first one I got all the way through, anyhow.
DOLLY: Fair dinkum?
ERROL: You see, I just got in. The company gave me a map and a bicycle and a train ticket to Mooro—Moo—roo—
DOLLY: Mooroopna.
ERROL: Thanks. I've never been so far from Melbourne.
DOLLY: So you're from the big smoke? What's it like?
ERROL: Good, I suppose. Just like anywhere. [*He looks around.*] There's picture theatres and municipal pools—
DOLLY: They have them here too, you know…

Except they're segregated. She moves away from him.

You go the way I told ya. On the other side of the railway line. You'll sell plenty of them encyclopedias there. Fancy coming to The Flats!
ERROL: Yes. But all's well that ends well.

DOLLY looks at him, puzzled. He couldn't possible mean her, could he?

I get to deliver them. In four weeks… [*Shyly*] Will you be around in four weeks, when I make my deliveries?
DOLLY: 'Spose. Not going anywhere.

He goes to put the book in the bicycle pannier but his bike is not there. A bicycle bell is heard offstage.

Not delivering them on ya bicycle, I hope?
ERROL: No… the company utility. Where is my bicycle?

DOLLY whistles extremely loudly.

DOLLY: [*in a loud blackfella accent*] Oi! You little monkeys, get that ruddy bicycle back 'ere, or I'll give youse a kick up the moom! [*Politely*] And you were worried about losing your map!

The sound of the bicycle being dropped offstage.

There it is. Well… goodbye, then.
ERROL: Goodbye, then… and thanks.
DOLLY: What for?

He stands and watches her while she returns to the humpy.

The lights go down then come up on the interior.

As DOLLY *enters,* GLADYS *puts down Errol's business card with a sigh, but remains transfixed by it.*

GLADYS: You're right, Mum.

DOLLY: What is she right about?

NAN DEAR: She's the cat's mother. And I'm right about everything.

NAN begins stoking up the fire.

DOLLY: [*chuckling*] He sure got a fright when his pushbike wasn't there.

GLADYS: Ester's boys took it for a spin?

DOLLY: Their legs could hardly reach the pedals. Lionel on the handlebars. Roy on the back and Robbie on the seat! Lad didn't seem to understand what a novelty a new Malvern Star is around here.

NAN DEAR: Come here, darling.

DOLLY dutifully goes over and gives NAN a hug.

You watch who you're mixing with. Hard to tell a good man from a bad. Bad one will promise you everything, then do the straight opposite, just like that.

NAN snaps her fingers and DOLLY repeats the gesture. GLADYS just rolls her eyes.

GLADYS: You get back to your books, Doll.

GLADYS looks at the card again.

DOLLY: But I need an encyclops to do me homework!

DOLLY squeals in mock horror as NAN chases her around inside the humpy with a wooden spoon.

GLADYS: Do you? [*To herself*] No… Silly woman.

But she puts the business card down the front of her dress.

The lights go down.

♦ ♦ ♦ ♦ ♦

SCENE THREE: LINO

DOLLY *is rummaging at the town tip. She looks at, and discards, a few items.*

The lights change to a dream sequence. A well-groomed SALESMAN *appears.*

SALESMAN: [*posh*] May I be of assistance, miss?
DOLLY: [*posh*] Why yars, I'm after new linoleum.
SALESMAN: We have a wide selection.
DOLLY: This pattern.
SALESMAN: Exquisite! Thank you for shopping at Daish's once more.

The lights change back to reality.

DOLLY *hoists the lino roll over her shoulder as the* SALESMAN *fades away.* DOLLY *walks past the cork trees. She sees someone in the shadows.*

COUSIN: [*offstage, slurring*] Hey, Dolores. You look real pretty today.
DOLLY: Hey, Leon.
COUSIN: [*offstage*] Why don't yah join us? We're having a bit of a party… You look like a party girl.
DOLLY: Nah, I'm busy. Nan's expecting me.
COUSIN: [*offstage*] 'Nother time then, Dolores.
DOLLY: Yeah, sure.
COUSIN: [*offstage*] Promise?
DOLLY: 'Course, cuz.

As DOLLY *staggers along* NAN *appears, going in the opposite direction.*

NAN DEAR: Good girl! [*Suspiciously*] Which way did you come?
DOLLY: Aren't you just glad I found it?
NAN DEAR: Yes… If I catch you going past those cork trees—
DOLLY: In good nick and all.
NAN DEAR: —mark my words, I'll wallop you.
DOLLY: Nan, I'm nearly seventeen. You can't scare me with 'boogey man' stories anymore. And besides, them goomees are harmless.
NAN DEAR: What you call them? Shame! They might be drinkers, but they're still our people.
DOLLY: [*to herself*] And model citizens to boot.
NAN DEAR: Show some respect, girl. They've had it hard, those lads.
DOLLY: How, Nan?
NAN DEAR: Never mind. They just have.
DOLLY: [*with a sigh*] Yes, Nan. [*Beat.*] Where's Mum?

NAN DEAR: Cannery. Wrangled another shift.
DOLLY: Why? What's she saving for?
NAN DEAR: Grown-up business.
DOLLY: Where you off to?
NAN DEAR: Spud Lane.
DOLLY: No need to ask what's for tea, then.

> NAN *exits and* DOLLY *staggers on, but when she sees* ERROL *leaning against the humpy wall, his bicycle nearby, she dumps the lino.*

It's you.
ERROL: I came to see your mother. About the encyclopedias.
DOLLY: Oh? Oh! But she won't be home for a bit.
ERROL: Really? I'll just have to wait. [*He planned it that way.*] It's a beautiful day.
DOLLY: It's stinking.
ERROL: It is hot… out here.

> *He eyes the humpy, but* DOLLY *won't acquiesce.*

You've been at school?
DOLLY: You ask a lot of questions.
ERROL: My dad reckons I ask too many. But now it's part of my job. They train me to ask questions.
DOLLY: Really?
ERROL: Do you mind if…?
DOLLY: Another question?
ERROL: May I have a glass of water?

> *He wipes his brow.* DOLLY *hesitates, then nods. He goes as if to enter.*

DOLLY: You can't come in… The… um… baby's sleeping.
ERROL: [*alarmed*] Baby? It's not…?
DOLLY: It's… it's my cousin's baby.

> *She goes in and quickly returns, barefoot, with a cup of water.* ERROL *looks at the tin cup with interest.*

ERROL: It's made out of a can!

> DOLLY *is humiliated but* ERROL *doesn't notice.*

How do you do that? You people can make something out of nothing.

He sees her reaction too late.

I, ah, I mean, I'm not trying to… to…
DOLLY: [*bitter*] 'You people'?
ERROL: I didn't mean… crikey Moses… It's fascinating. [*Beat.*] Is it a little girl?
DOLLY: Pardon?
ERROL: The baby.
DOLLY: Oh, ah, ye—Ah, no, a boy.

She softens at his interest.

ERROL: Would you like to go for a ride?

She is uncertain but hops on the bike. It wasn't what he had in mind… he was thinking for a dink. She rides around in a figure-eight and he trots to keep up with her. She starts to hum a popular song and after a while he joins in with the words.

DOLLY: [*shyly*] Is it good selling encyclopedias?
ERROL: Sure. I'm out and about—free. I meet all sorts of people. What about you? What will you do when you leave school?
DOLLY: Pick.
ERROL: Pick?
DOLLY: You know, fruit… Or the Blue Moon.

ERROL *is puzzled.*

The cannery. [*Beat.*] Maybe the hospital…
ERROL: Hospital?
DOLLY: Well, who knows…?
ERROL: You should come to the city. There's swags of work. And you'd like the city.
DOLLY: Would I? Nan wouldn't like that. City's are full of sin.

ERROL *laughs.*

Anyway, what would I do?
ERROL: [*boldly*] What do you want to do? A girl like you… you could do anything you want.
DOLLY: You sound like my mum.
ERROL: She must be smart.

DOLLY *shrugs, both proud and embarrassed.*

DOLLY: She's…

ERROL: What?

DOLLY: Never mind. [*Beat.*] I'd like to be a model, like in the magazines, or an actress, like Gina Lollobrigida... She's so... so... well, you know... [*sexy...*] But really, I... it's silly, but I'd kind of like to be a nurse.

> *She's dreamy.*

ERROL: That's not silly... Nurse Dolly.

DOLLY: But Mum reckons I'm good with figures—you know, algebra. Of course you know. But what could I do with that?

ERROL: Why, lots—

> *But he doesn't get a chance to tell her, as* GLADYS *appears with a crappy old bookcase balanced on the old pram.* ERROL *leaps over to help her.*

GLADYS: [*loudly*] We'll be needing one of these, eh, Errol?

> ERROL *holds his finger up to his mouth.*

ERROL: Baby's asleep.

GLADYS: Baby?

DOLLY: [*firmly*] Cousin's baby.

> GLADYS *nods, a little puzzled. She pats the bookcase.*

GLADYS: Good old Daish's. Actually, I thought I saw you on the other side, Dolly.

ERROL: Daish's?

DOLLY: [*warning her*] Mum.

GLADYS: It's the tip.

> DOLLY *shoots her a glare but* GLADYS *has a head of steam and keeps going.*

It should have been where they built us housing, being the highest land around here... but, oh no, they decided to turn it into the town tip... [*uncertain*] actually.

> *They watch* DOLLY *go inside, humiliated.*

I'm sorry. You don't need to hear—

ERROL: It's okay.

> *They are both embarrassed.* ERROL *turns his attention to the bookcase.*

Just needs a lick of paint.

GLADYS: That's what I thought.

> *Triumphantly she pulls an obviously used and bashed can from the pram.* GLADYS *laughs and* ERROL *joins in.*
>
> *The lights go down.*

♦ ♦ ♦ ♦ ♦

SCENE FOUR: HOUSE OF BIBA

GLADYS *serves out the stew while* DOLLY *sets the table.*

NAN DEAR: You haven't set a spot for Papa Dear.

DOLLY: What's the point?

NAN DEAR: Just do it.

DOLLY: It's been three months.

NAN DEAR: He's busy doing good work. God's work and hard work.

GLADYS: I heard he's in Western Australia. Touring the communities there. Doll, did you see that photograph that he sent over? It was in the newspaper and all. [*Beat.*] He could walk through that door any day now.

> *The lights change for a dream sequence.* PAPA DEAR, *in old-fashioned hat and coat, dances in, throws his hat on the hatstand, kisses* GLADYS *on the top of the head, and dances out. No one takes any notice of him but* GLADYS, *who smiles at him warmly.*

Papa Dear…

DOLLY: Okay, okay… an empty place for Papa Dear. [*To herself*] Just as well he likes potatoes.

> *She sets another place and they begin to eat.*

[*To* NAN] Potato stew tonight, Nan? What a surprise!

NAN DEAR: [*warning her*] Cheeky…

DOLLY: Mum, there's a summer job going at Trevaks that I could try for. They teach you the cash register. And I could maybe get offcuts for you to sew, Nan! I know I could do it.

GLADYS: Of course you could!

NAN DEAR: You'll be at the Blue Moon. With us. As usual.

GLADYS: [*hopefully*] But it sounds like a good job… a good opportunity…

But NAN *will brook no argument. She shakes her head and that's that.*

NAN DEAR: It's a bit chilly tonight, go get me a cardie, Doll.

> DOLLY *leaves the room. As soon as she's out of sight,* NAN *hisses at* GLADYS.

They're never going to give her that job.

GLADYS: She's good with figures.

NAN DEAR: A girl from The Flats? I don't even see the town Aboriginals working in stores.

GLADYS: Why should her address stop her in life?

NAN DEAR: Gladys, get a grip.

GLADYS: [*to herself*] I'm trying, Mum, I'm trying.

> *Hurt, she turns the radio on.* DOLLY *returns with the cardigan that she puts around* NAN'*s shoulders.*

DOLLY DYER: [*radio voice-over*] … only Ajax with the miracle foaming action cleans so quick, works so easily and polishes so bright.

BOB DYER: [*radio voice-over*] You sound like one of the elves in the commercial. Very good. Cleans so easy…

NAN DEAR: Elves, cash registers… That's exactly what I'm talking about.

> *She looks at* GLADYS *accusingly.*

♦♦♦♦♦

SCENE FIVE: THE DELIVERY

Interior of the humpy.

DOLLY *and* ERROL *look slightly more mature than their earlier scene together.* DOLLY *is really embarrassed that* GLADYS *has allowed* ERROL *into the humpy.*

DOLLY: [*whispering*] But why do you have to do it in here?

GLADYS: It's ready to storm out there… Volume A would get wet.

> GLADYS *turns her attention to a brown-paper parcel.* NAN *is holding back. Throughout, she is openly hostile to* ERROL.

Cuppa, Errol?

ERROL: Actually, I'd love a cup of coffee if you've got one, Mrs Banks. But, first, don't you want to see it, in all its glory?

GLADYS: Coffee? Coffee, you say? [*She gestures for* DOLLY *to come closer. Whispering*] Dolly, nick next door to Uncle's and see if he has a jar of coffee. Hurry up. [*To* ERROL] Coffee won't be a moment, lad. Oh, and it nearly slipped my mind, the down payment. We'd better sort that out first. Dolly, get down the jam tins, will you please?

    DOLLY *passes* GLADYS *the jam tins, one at a time.*

Now. Pear money, peach-picking money, tomatoes—hardly anything in that tin, not worth picking them at tuppence for ten pound. Only bonus is they give you the bruised ones.

    DOLLY *glares at* GLADYS *who is oblivious.*

NAN DEAR: The bruised ones that otherwise go to the pigs.

    GLADYS *carefully empties each tin and counts up the coins. (She knows exactly how much is in each tin.)* DOLLY *hands* GLADYS *the last of the jars.*

GLADYS: Not that jar, Dolly, that's your glory-box stash.

    DOLLY *looks embarrassed. She exits.*

Orange money—don't like picking them, don't like getting up them ladders one bit.

NAN DEAR: At least you're clear of the snakes up there.

ERROL: Snakes?

GLADYS: Always snakes in paddocks. Once when Dolly was a babe in a wooden box, tea towel over her to keep off the sun—and come smoko I went to feed her and there was this massive carpet snake curled up with her! And my Dolly was fast asleep! Not a peep out of her! She was a good baby.

ERROL: And it didn't bite her or anything?

    They look at him askance.

NAN DEAR: [*to herself*] It was a mamel.

GLADYS: A carpet snake, love.

    ERROL *doesn't comprehend.* DOLLY *returns and busies herself making the hot drinks.*

ERROL: Oh? But you killed it anyway?

NAN DEAR: [*to herself*] Killed it! Encyclops boy and he knows nothing!

> DOLLY *sniggers.*

GLADYS: They keep down the mice. Anyway… two pounds six shillings deposit. Six shillings every three months for twenty-four months, that's the deal.

DOLLY: Oh, and here's the contract all filled in.

> *She hands the contract to* ERROL *who scans it.*

ERROL: And signed by you, Mrs Banks?

GLADYS: Done!

> ERROL *looks slightly puzzled, but then gets excited.*

ERROL: Done! Not my first sale, but surely my longest negotiation. Six months! Now… drum roll please…

GLADYS: Oh, I'm so excited!

> *He hands over the parcel and* GLADYS *tears it open. She opens the book—celestial music is heard. She touches the pages lovingly, then holds the book out for* DOLLY. DOLLY *has to first hand* GLADYS *and* ERROL *their cuppas.*

Isn't it… extraordinary… daught? Volume A! Would you look at the pictures? In colour too! Coffee okay, son?

> ERROL *takes a quick sip and nearly gags.*

ERROL: Just lovely, ma'am.

> NAN *just scowls.* GLADYS *puts Volume A pride of place in the middle of her new bookcase.*

GLADYS: Call me Aunty, Errol. I imagine we'll be seeing a bit of you.

> *She looks from* ERROL *to* DOLLY *and back again.* DOLLY *looks embarrassed.* NAN *scowls even more.*

When he comes to pick up the payments.

NAN DEAR: You mean you've got to pay more for those things?

> *The lights go down then come straight up again.*
>
> DOLLY, *outside the humpy, is leaning against the wall, while* ERROL *fumbles with his keys.*

ERROL: Miss Banks…

DOLLY: Dolly. We're not too fussed about fancy titles.
ERROL: Dolly…
DOLLY: Yes?
ERROL: Dolly… That's a pretty name.
DOLLY: It's Dolores, actually.
ERROL: Really? That's pretty too…

> DOLLY *moves away slightly, and* ERROL *quickly speaks to hold her attention. But she was only getting a piece of wattle gum to chew.*

Um… Do you like music? Oh, I'm sure you do. [*Curious*] What's that?

DOLLY: Snooty goggles.

> *She gives him a piece to chew.*

ERROL: Snooty…?
DOLLY: Goggles.
ERROL: Hmmm…
DOLLY: If you don't like it…
ERROL: But it's interesting.

> GLADYS *opens the door and sweeps some dirt outside, studiously ignoring the young 'ens.*

[*Nervously*] Er… I was thinking… Dolores…

> GLADYS *makes encouraging motions at him.*

DOLLY: Really?
ERROL: Yes.

> ERROL *looks sideways at* GLADYS, *who pointedly goes back inside.*

Why do you live out here?
DOLLY: Where else would we live?
ERROL: In town?
DOLLY: Nan likes to be near all the other families. And Mum does too but—
ERROL: The other families…?
DOLLY: You ask a lot of questions. Can't you find the answers in there?

> *She points to the encyclopedia.*

ERROL: [*grinning*] Not the answers to the questions I want to ask. Like...
DOLLY: Yes?
ERROL: Like... [*In a rush*] There's a dance on in Shepparton next Saturday...
DOLLY: True?
ERROL: There is. With a band playing... a good band...
DOLLY: How do you know that? You seen 'em? You heard 'em?
ERROL: No, actually. [*Pause.*] You do like music?
DOLLY: Already told you that.
ERROL: 'Cos I was thinking...
DOLLY: You were thinking...
ERROL: If I organised my schedule... Well, funnily enough, I already have, and I was thinking...
DOLLY: Yes, thinking...
ERROL: Which means I happen to be in Shepparton on Saturday. Which means...
DOLLY: It means...?
ERROL: That I'm available... and if you're available...
DOLLY: Available...
ERROL: And interested...
DOLLY: Yes... yes... go on...
ERROL: Well, I'd be most pleased if you would—

> GLADYS *bursts out of the humpy.*

GLADYS: Oh, for heaven's sake, spit it out, will ya, son?! [*To* DOLLY] He wants to invite you to the dance.
DOLLY: Mum!
ERROL: Mrs Banks!
NAN DEAR: [*from inside, loudly*] Glaaadys!

> GLADYS *hurries inside.* DOLLY *moves up very close to* ERROL*'s face.*

ERROL: So will you? Will you go with me?
DOLLY: Listen, fella. Do you have any idea what'll happen if you walk into that dance with me?
ERROL: Uh, no... [*Worried*] Is there some other bloke on the scene? Is that it? Will some fella want to punch me on the nose for sweet-talking his girl?

DOLLY: You're white. I'm Aboriginal. Or haven't you noticed?
ERROL: Well, yes… but…
DOLLY: I'm from The Flats. Not even one of those townie types of cross-over Aboriginals.
ERROL: What matters is you. Not your address…
DOLLY: That's sweet.

> DOLLY *visibly softens towards him.*

NAN DEAR: [*from inside, yelling*] Dolly!
DOLLY: Go! You'll get us in trouble.
ERROL: Who with?

> DOLLY *starts to move away but he grabs her hands and slowly they move into a jitterbug, dancing perfectly together. We hear the song 'A Girl Like You' by Cliff Richard and the Shadows.*

You're going to come with me, then?

> DOLLY *knows their relationship cannot work.*

DOLLY: No… it's… impossible.

> *But he pulls her back towards him.*

ERROL: Nothing's impossible. Can I pick you up from here?

> *She shakes her head.*

Then I'll meet you halfway.
DOLLY: With your sense of direction?
ERROL: There's these gnarled trees down the track.
DOLLY: The cork trees.
ERROL: All twisty and rough.
DOLLY: I know them.
ERROL: That can be our special meeting spot!
DOLLY: I'm not sure.
ERROL: It's here—or it's there. What'll it be?

> DOLLY *hesitates.*

DOLLY: I'll meet you at the hall.
ERROL: And I'll bring you home? Swell.
DOLLY: Swell.

> *He swings her away… There is a sound of the door being opened, and* DOLLY *swings out of his reach.*

NAN *appears and the music stops suddenly, as if the record has been scratched, and the mood is broken.*

DOLLY *goes in without a word.* NAN *looks daggers at* ERROL.

NAN DEAR: It's getting dark. Very dark. Time for you to move on. Take the short cut, past the cork trees.

She moves inside and slams the door.

The lights fade.

♦ ♦ ♦ ♦ ♦

SCENE SIX: THE INSPECTION

NAN *and* GLADYS *are inside the humpy, straightening everything in sight with a nervous, anxious energy.*

NAN DEAR: [*whispering*] I'm worried about Ester.

GLADYS: Send Doll over.

The two women stand up—as if at attention—as the INSPECTOR, *a well-dressed white man, steps back into the front room.*

INSPECTOR: I say, crocheted pillow shams. Such beautiful work!

GLADYS: That would be my mother's handiwork.

INSPECTOR: And your name is…?

GLADYS: Mrs Banks.

INSPECTOR: And…?

GLADYS: My mother, Mrs Dear.

The INSPECTOR *is writing notes.*

INSPECTOR: [*pleasant, but distracted*] Is there a Mr Banks?

GLADYS: Deceased. He fought in the war.

INSPECTOR: Is there a Mr Dear?

GLADYS: Yes, Papa Dear.

INSPECTOR: And he is where, at present? At work?

GLADYS: Why, yes. In the Western District, I believe.

INSPECTOR: Away shearing?

NAN DEAR: He's a pastor. Our own pastor.

INSPECTOR: Pastor Dear? I do believe I have heard of him. He does good works among your community.

NAN DEAR: Yes.

GLADYS: He's very well-known…

But he's moved across the room and GLADYS *is unsure whether to continue that line of conversation.*

INSPECTOR: It must be quite unpleasant here in summer?
GLADYS: Excuse me?
INSPECTOR: The heat.
GLADYS: It's bearable. Better than winter.
INSPECTOR: Oh?
GLADYS: Because of the floods.
INSPECTOR: How frequently does it flood?
GLADYS: [*unsure*] Oh, now and then. Now and then.
INSPECTOR: So, only the two back rooms… Are there children staying with you?
GLADYS: My children are all grown up, off working—

At that moment DOLLY *bursts in, as if she has something urgent to say.* NAN *is gesticulating for* DOLLY *to shoo.*

NAN DEAR: [*whispering*] Give Ester a hand.

But DOLLY *has been spotted.*

GLADYS: Except for my daughter.

The INSPECTOR *appraises* DOLLY.

INSPECTOR: And she is…?
GLADYS: Dolores. Dolores Alice Banks. She's just back from the high school. She's currently undertaking her [*with a hint of triumph*] Leaving Certificate.

For the first time he turns his full attention to the women.

INSPECTOR: Really? That's the way! And what does the future hold for you, Dolores?
DOLLY: Well, I'd like to work at the hospital—
GLADYS: —as a bookkeeper—
NAN DEAR: —in the laundry.

The INSPECTOR *is not sure if they're having a go at him or not. He notices the floor.*

INSPECTOR: Linoleum?
NAN DEAR: Yes.
GLADYS: From Daish's.

INSPECTOR: I'm not familiar with the department stores around these parts.

> DOLLY *has to put her hand over her mouth to suppress a giggle. The* INSPECTOR *looks out the humpy window. He clasps his hands together, his 'tour' completed.*

Well! I don't know how you do it. Your whites are so white! With river water, no less!

GLADYS: Just boiled up in a kero tin, with Velvet soap and a blue bag, same as everyone.

INSPECTOR: Yes... As a result of my report, things will change, Mrs Banks. Things must change. The sanitation arrangements for one.

> GLADYS *and* NAN *exchange worried looks.*

And you need interim housing to ease you into the townships. Are you aware of the concept of assimilation, Mrs Banks?

> GLADYS *isn't sure how to respond, or even if a response is required.*

GLADYS: Yes, but we—

> *But* NAN *elbows her.*

INSPECTOR: The Aborigine needs to be absorbed into the community. But how can he be absorbed until he learns to live like us? I will recommend assimilation, in my report. It is a vexed issue, to be sure, but someone must take leadership. First, the housing problem must be fixed... After all, how can the children study in the evenings if there is no electric light?

GLADYS: [*unsure*] Yes.

INSPECTOR: Yes. I will do all I can. But... in the meantime, you need to rally yourselves. Speak to your local MPs. Form a delegation. Collect petitions. Write letters. Inform yourself. Knowledge is power, ladies.

GLADYS: [*hesitantly*] Yes. [*More assured*] Yes.

INSPECTOR: Thank you for the cuppa, Mrs Dear. Mmm... something smells delicious?

NAN DEAR: It's just damper.

GLADYS: Please help yourself.

INSPECTOR: Marvellous! Quite a treat, fresh damper. Thank you.

NAN DEAR: Yes.

GLADYS: Do come again.

> NAN *elbows* GLADYS. *The* INSPECTOR *exits.* GLADYS *rubs where* NAN *elbowed her.*

NAN DEAR: [*disgusted*] 'Do come again!'
GLADYS: My Lordy, I was nervous.
DOLLY: What is he here for? Why is he checking us out? And who is he?
NAN DEAR: Never you mind.

> *She is peeking out the window, checking out which way he is going.*

DOLLY: Nan, why do you always treat me like a child?
GLADYS: [*low*] That man, he's writing a report. About the way we live. For the Government of Victoria.
DOLLY: A report? Like a mark out of one hundred?
GLADYS: Something like that.
DOLLY: Will they build us our own houses, like you're always on about?
GLADYS: Perhaps.

> NAN *snorts.*

DOLLY: Do you still want me to go over to Aunty Ester's?
NAN DEAR: [*sadly*] Probably too late now.

> *Beat.*

DOLLY: Nan? What's wrong, Nan?

> NAN *shakes her head and vanishes outside to hide the anxiety she is feeling.* GLADYS *watches* DOLLY *watching her.*

GLADYS: [*falsely bright*] So how was school today, Dolly?
DOLLY: Same as every day… Mum! Nancy was talking about a ball that's coming up. The Miss Mooroopna-Shepparton Ball! Mum?

> GLADYS *has not been listening.* NAN *returns and shakes her head at* GLADYS*'s inquiring look.*

GLADYS: Well then, Dolly—haven't you got sums to do?
DOLLY: Yeah, so I can be a bookkeeper… in the laundry.

> DOLLY *scoots out of reach but* NAN *doesn't even try to smack her. The two older women look at each other, then in the direction* DOLLY *has gone, worried.*

GLADYS: They won't take her.

NAN DEAR: She's seventeen. They'd make her work for someone. Like they did you.

GLADYS: I think he was impressed at her schooling.

NAN DEAR: Maybe. And how clean it was?

GLADYS: Definitely. Oh, Mum… But I'd like to see that report of his— I'd like to know what he says about us.

NAN DEAR: [*an outburst*] And what bloody good would that do?! Daydreams!

Crankily, she thumps the radio to life.

GLADYS: [*to herself*] They're not really daydreams…

Because she intends to make them come true.

♦ ♦ ♦ ♦ ♦

SCENE SEVEN: THE TURN

Early evening.

DOLLY, *out of sight, is singing to the radio.* NAN *sits in the only chair, cleaning a pair of slingback shoes with white shoe cleaner. She is acutely aware of what is happening around her.* GLADYS *is fussing around getting ready, and also singing—but a different song.*

GLADYS: My white gloves?

NAN DEAR: Tomato box by the bed.

GLADYS: You need a cuppa, Mum? [*Louder*] Get a wriggle on, Dolly.

NAN DEAR: Full up to pussy's bow.

DOLLY: Where's the talcum powder?

NAN DEAR: Trough.

DOLLY: Thanks, Nan. Can I use a little of your lavender water? Thanks. You got your glasses, Nan?

NAN DEAR: Right here, love.

GLADYS: Mum, you sure you don't want to come to Aunty's? Did I mention it's a housing fundraiser?

NAN DEAR: You did. Why else would you make rock cakes all afternoon?

GLADYS: Just six dozen. It's my little contribution. See, Uncle's planning to negotiate for Daish's, in a 'new deal'. They've got in mind Aboriginal housing. They want to call the housing Rumbalara. It means—

NAN DEAR: I know what it means.

GLADYS: —'end of the rainbow'. Sounds beaut, doesn't it, this 'new deal'? They say the houses'll have running water…

The lights change for GLADYS*'s dream sequence.*

A tap appears from nowhere and from it flows blue jewels in an approximation of water. NAN*'s words break in and bring the fantasy to an end as the lights change back to reality.*

NAN DEAR: But Daish's is the town tip. They already decided that in '47.

GLADYS: He's—we're—going to have another go at it. I might even go on the committee.

NAN DEAR: You? Don't ever get too clever, my girl.

GLADYS: Just a thought.

NAN DEAR: You get knocked down when you get too clever.

GLADYS: Yes, Mum. I'll get you comfy with the radio.

She fiddles with the radio.

RADIO ANNOUNCER: [*voice-over*] Ajax foaming cleaner. Because Ajax contains bleach, you'll stop paying the elbow tax…

NAN DEAR: Honestly, they're mad about whiteness.

GLADYS *belts the radio and it reverts to soothing country and western music.*

GLADYS: You got your crochet hook, Mum?

NAN DEAR: Stop fussing.

GLADYS: Dolly, would you like to borrow the girdle? That dress—

DOLLY *walks in, looking gorgeous in a very tight-waisted 1950s dress.*

NAN DEAR: —that dress never looked like that on you.

GLADYS: A vision! My baby…

She twirls DOLLY *around, proud as.*

NAN DEAR: She doesn't look like a baby.

GLADYS: I'm off now, Mum, unless there's anything…?

NAN *shoos her away.*

You look beautiful, Dolores. Truly beautiful. [*Whispering*] Have a lovely time… with Errol.

GLADYS *gives* DOLLY *a peck on the cheek and exits.* NAN, *once she's gone, rushes over and gets the latest volume of the encyclopedia to look at. She settles back in her chair and notices that* DOLLY *is still there.*

NAN DEAR: Aren't you going with her?

DOLLY: [*evasive*] Ah, no. I'm getting a lift. On account of Aunty's shoes.

DOLLY *puts on earrings and fiddles with her hair.*

NAN DEAR: [*suspiciously*] All this fuss for a little bush concert?

DOLLY: I'm not going to the fundraiser.

NAN DEAR: You're not? Then where, pray tell?

DOLLY: To a dance. In Shepparton.

NAN DEAR: Your mother know this? Of course—she's in on it. Who's going to be at this dance?

DOLLY: The usual.

NAN DEAR: Who's bringing you home? One of your cousins? At least Gladys would have made sure you were brought home safe.

DOLLY: Errol's bringing me home.

NAN DEAR: That encyclops boy? That gubba fella?

DOLLY: Mm-mm. Errol Fisher.

NAN DEAR: He's Errol Fisher? A Fisher?

DOLLY *sighs.*

He'll be there?

DOLLY: Everyone's going to be there! It's a dance, Nan.

NAN *goes into a coughing fit. As* DOLLY *rushes to get her a glass of water,* NAN *hides the white shoes.*

You right, Nan?

NAN DEAR: I'm chilly.

DOLLY *gets* NAN *a blanket and arranges it over her knees.*

You get going, then… My crochet hook?

DOLLY: I'm sure you had it… Here it is! Nan, have you seen those shoes?

NAN DEAR: Aren't they under Glad's bed?

DOLLY *disappears then reappears shaking her head.*

DOLLY: [*panicking*] What time is it?

DOLLY *finds the shoes under the chair. There's a truck honking outside and* DOLLY *rushes to the window.* NAN *coughs again.* DOLLY*'s concerned.*

NAN DEAR: Parched… But you'd better be off … Go out, kick up your heels, love… Don't mind me here all alone.

DOLLY *fills up her mug from the billy.*

DOLLY: You sure?

NAN DEAR: Though I do feel like a serve of swan eggs…

DOLLY: Swan eggs? You're okay, aren't you, Nan?

NAN *coughs.* DOLLY *looks from the source of the honking to* NAN. *The honking is more insistent. The coughing is more wracking.* DOLLY *opens the door and disappears.*

NAN *rushes over to the window, then rushes back and settles herself back in her chair. As* DOLLY *returns inside (waving sadly to the departing truck)* NAN *looks relieved, then remembers to cough again.*

NAN DEAR: Come here, love.

DOLLY *dutifully goes over and gives* NAN *a hug.* DOLLY *removes her accessories.* NAN *perks up.*

DOLLY: Okay now, Nan?

NAN DEAR: So, so.

DOLLY *strokes* NAN*'s hair tenderly.*

Perhaps I will go to the concert, a little later on. A few hymns would be lovely. You can walk me over, Dolly. There'll be a few young 'ens there. Heard there's a nice Wemba Wemba boy down from Swan Hill…

DOLLY *hugs her, disappointed in missing the dance.*

DOLLY: We're probably related to him too, eh, Nan?

NAN DEAR: We'll find someone for you. Go on, put on your earrings, love.

The lights go down.

♦♦♦♦♦

SCENE EIGHT: WASHING-DAY BLUES

As the lights come up, NAN *is wringing out the whites, then hanging them on the old-fashioned clothes line (no pegs).* DOLLY, *dragging her feet as she walks home from school, wordlessly plonks down her bag and gives her a hand.*

DOLLY: Nan, Robbie wasn't at school today. Neither was Lionel or Roy.

NAN DEAR: Yes.

DOLLY: It's 'cos of that inspector, ay, Nan?

NAN DEAR: [*harshly*] Don't listen to gossip, Dolores.

DOLLY: Is that why Aunty Ester's down at the cork trees, drinkin' with the goo—?

NAN DEAR: Don't speak ill, girl.

DOLLY: But is it 'cos they took her boys?

> NAN *shoots her a look of warning.*

I want to know. I'm not a child. I'm a woman, Nan.

> NAN *will not answer.* DOLLY *turns on the radio.*

RADIO ANNOUNCER: [*voice-over*] And in other news, well-known Melbourne vocalist and teenage idol of thousands, Ernie Sigley, will sing with the Echuca Rhythm Kings orchestra at the inaugural Miss Mooroopna-Shepparton Ball. So, girls, put on your prettiest frocks, and be there… And now here's Lucky Lennie's…

DOLLY: The Miss Mooroopna-Shepparton Ball…

> *There's longing in her voice.* NAN *goes to get another load of washing from the kero tin.* GLADYS *hurries up the track towards them.*

GLADYS: Dolly! There's a trainee program, at the bank, in town. I heard Nancy Woolthorpe's mother talking about it when I was at the butcher's.

NAN DEAR: When you're the last to be served, you hear lots of things.

DOLLY: And?

GLADYS: And? You'll go for it. If Nancy's going for it, you can.

DOLLY: What do you want from me, Mum? Do you want me to walk like them, talk like them, wear a twin-set like them? Pretend to be one of them?

GLADYS: Are you finished?

DOLLY: No. And yet we live like this… out here.

NAN DEAR: At least here we sink or swim on our own. Not like the Cummeragunja days, always at the mercy of the manager—

She stops abruptly, a little shamed by her outburst. DOLLY *is pleased that* NAN *has revealed a little info. But* GLADYS *has something to say.*

GLADYS: You ask me what I want. Well, I want what any mother, black, white or brindle, wants for her daughter. That's all.

GLADYS *stares at them defiantly, before she goes into the humpy.*

DOLLY: Nan…why don't we have a normal life?

NAN DEAR: This is normal—

DOLLY: Getting flooded all the time—

NAN DEAR: It's just the way it is. That's nature.

DOLLY: But why? It's like we're fighting nature all the time. Living on the riverbank—

NAN DEAR: You're the one who's fighting. You and your mother. Fighting against how things are.

DOLLY: What's wrong with that? Papa Dear fights for things to get better.

DOLLY *sighs, resigned. They continue to hang up the washing.*

It's not going to rain, is it?

NAN DEAR: Would I be doing this if it was about to rain? [*Beat.*] All these questions, questions, questions…

DOLLY: Yes, Nan. But how come there's no answers?

Beat.

NAN DEAR: A ball.

DOLLY *is surprised that* NAN *has revived the topic.*

DOLLY: Not just any ball. The Miss Mooroopna-Shepparton Ball.

NAN DEAR: Is it just for Aboriginals?

DOLLY: No.

NAN DEAR: That boy's not going to be there? That encyclops boy?

DOLLY: Doubt it… [*She waits, then buries her face in a white sheet.*] 'Your whites are so white, Mrs Dear.'

NAN DEAR: As if that were the be-all and end-all. As if that were the bloody be-all and end-all. [*Beat*.] All right.

DOLLY: All right, what?

NAN DEAR: You can go.

DOLLY: I can? To the ball? And enter the competition? Yipee! You'll make me a new dress, Nan? A really gorgeous one with lots of fabric—pretty fabric.

NAN DEAR: Maybe.

DOLLY: Please, Nan.

NAN DEAR: Yes. Yes.

>   DOLLY *dances around* NAN.

Haven't you got something to do instead of getting under people's feet, girl?

DOLLY: I could get the water?

NAN DEAR: You go and play. While you're still a child. Git.

DOLLY: Thanks, Nan. A big skirt. And a peplum.

NAN: Peplum?

DOLLY: Like in the picture on the wall. Love you, Nan.

>   DOLLY *hugs her.*

NAN DEAR: Don't get your hopes up. It's not the House of Biba, you know. Go on, git.

>   *The lights go down.*

♦ ♦ ♦ ♦ ♦

SCENE NINE: HOME SWEET HOME

As the lights come up, GLADYS *is going around the humpy emptying the mouse traps of dead mice and setting new traps, while* DOLLY *does her homework. A song is heard on the radiogram: 'I'll Be Home' by Pat Boone.*

GLADYS: First hint of cold weather and they're in, like a flash.

>   DOLLY *sings a line from the song.*

I made another payment today.

>   DOLLY *glances up and sees another volume of the encyclopedia is on the bookcase.*

DOLLY: Up to K. I'll be nineteen by the time we're up to Z.

> DOLLY *goes over and gets down the latest volume and pours over it.*

GLADYS: You do think they're wonderful, though? You're 'expanding your possibilities'?

DOLLY: Of course, Mum. Every day I learn something new about the big, wide world. That see-through section with the body—the muscles, and the bones, and the veins—that's my favourite. I love reading about the gizzards.

GLADYS: My… gizzards. That makes it all worthwhile.

DOLLY: [*casually*] So you saw…

GLADYS: [*equally casual*] He inquired after you.

DOLLY: He did?

> GLADYS *picks up a mouse that is still alive.*

GLADYS: I'll let this one go in the scrub.

DOLLY: So it can just find its way back here?

> GLADYS *vanishes outside with the mouse and* DOLLY, *restless, checks out her reflection in a small cracked piece of mirror.* GLADYS *returns.*

[*Casually*] Errol…?

GLADYS: Oh, yes, he was sorry he missed you the other week. He happened to ask if you were attending this ball coming up. And I said, yes, by coincidence, you were!

DOLLY: So what else did he say?

GLADYS: He asked if he could meet you at your 'special spot'. Asked. Real polite. Now, don't mind Nan—it'll be our little secret. What she won't know—

DOLLY: —won't hurt her. Except—Nan already said I could go. She's making me a dress. With a peplum.

She points to a picture of a peplum on the wall.

GLADYS: [*annoyed*] Did she just? And why was it her place to give you permission?

DOLLY: Mum!

GLADYS: Well, it's not right. I'm the mother.

DOLLY: Yes, [*exaggerating*] Mum. [*Dreamily*] So we ren-des-vous [*rhyming with booze*]—

GLADYS: If you spent more time on your French, and less time staring at peplums, you'd know it's pronounced 'rendezvous'.
DOLLY: [*angrily*] You think you know everything—
GLADYS: I don't—
DOLLY: Too right, you don't.
GLADYS: [*quietly*] Don't speak to me like that.
DOLLY: You going to wash out my mouth with soap? Nan thinks soap and water, and you think that books and school, are the answer to everything.
GLADYS: You're not too old for a wattle stick across your bare legs.
DOLLY: You've never hit me in your life.

>   DOLLY *and* GLADYS *are locked in a staring match.*

It's me that gets stones thrown at her when I walk down the street. It's me that gets snide remarks.
GLADYS: You think I haven't had my fair share? Or Nan? Even Papa Dear—not even he escapes it. Don't think he doesn't get put in his place. [*Beat.*] You have to learn not to let them shame you.
DOLLY: Have you, Mum? Have you learnt not to be shamed by them? [*Beat.*] I thought not. You're always telling me to stick up for myself, but when do you, eh?

>   *A long pause.* DOLLY *exits.* NAN *enters.* GLADYS *vents her frustration.*

GLADYS: [*angrily*] Re this ball, why are you saying if she can step out? She's my daughter. I have brought up three others before her.
NAN DEAR: Boys, Gladys. Girls are a different kettle of fish.

>   *Beat.*

GLADYS: I'll make the decisions regarding Dolores, thank you.
NAN DEAR: Then do it.
GLADYS: I have. She's going to the ball. And Errol Fisher is walking her home.
NAN DEAR: But—
GLADYS: No.

>   NAN *goes to protest further but holds her tongue when she sees the look on* GLADYS*'s face.*

♦ ♦ ♦ ♦ ♦

SCENE TEN: THE BANK VS MRS BANKS

The interior of a BANK MANAGER*'s office.*

GLADYS, *who's all dressed up, is sitting in the visitor's seat while the* BANK MANAGER *sits behind his desk.*

BANK MANAGER: And how can I be of service, Mrs…?
GLADYS: Banks. Mrs Len Banks.
BANK MANAGER: Mrs Banks. You're inquiring about a loan, perhaps?
GLADYS: Oh, no. It's about my youngest, Dolly.

>GLADYS *rummages in her bag.*

BANK MANAGER: And she…?
GLADYS: Pardon?

>*She triumphantly produces a photo of* DOLLY. *The* BANK MANAGER *puts on his glasses and studies the photo.*

BANK MANAGER: Yes. Very pretty face. [*Beat.*] But I'm still not sure why you're here…
GLADYS: The teller's position, of course.
BANK MANAGER: I don't think so…
GLADYS: But she's just completed her Leaving Certificate—the first in the family—with real good grades… 'N' top of her class in algebra…

>*Her earnest dialogue is hardly heard as we hear* DOLLY, *who becomes visible behind the gauze, picking fruit in an orchard and singing the chorus of 'Catch a Falling Star'.*

>*On the* BANK MANAGER*'s desk is a tray with two china cups of tea, milk jug and sugar bowl. He pours a cup for himself, but doesn't offer one to* GLADYS. *As the song ends, and the image behind the gauze fades, we return to* GLADYS*'s words.*

… She'd be a fine asset. Here's her school report—see, all As and Bs—and she won this for best and fairest for women's basketball…

>*She hands over the report and a ribbon.*

BANK MANAGER: Well, it's all very impressive… What I'm wondering is how she'd fit in.
GLADYS: [*steely*] She'd fit in fine.

BANK MANAGER: In a job such as this, reliability is important... I wondering how would she get into town each day.
GLADYS: She has a bicycle. She's on time for school. Look... [*She pulls out of her bag a special certificate for punctuality.*] For punctuality.
BANK MANAGER: Splendid. Now, rapport with our customers is important—sorry, rapport means—
GLADYS: [*through gritted teeth*] —getting along. Making people feel comfortable, like.
BANK MANAGER: Yes. [*Beat.*] Mrs Banks, are you a customer of this bank?
GLADYS: Well, no. [*Confessing*] I've never even been in one of these before.
BANK MANAGER: A bank manager's office?
GLADYS: A bank!
BANK MANAGER: But everyone needs savings...

> *From his drawer, he produces a tin money bank and a passbook and hands them over to* GLADYS.

You put your pennies in here, when they add up to a pound, you bring them in to us and we write the amount in your savings book. It helps you to save for something special, and you know that your money is safe.
GLADYS: Just like jam tins.
BANK MANAGER: Just like jam tins.

> GLADYS *looks at the tin then, seeing the* BANK MANAGER'*s gesture, she gets out her purse. He indicates to her that payment is not needed and she puts the tin in her bag. They both smile weakly.*

Well, if that's all...

> *He stands up, as if their business has concluded.*

DOLLY: [*voice-over echo*] Have you learnt not to be shamed by them? Eh?
GLADYS: No. The trainee position. For my Dolly.
BANK MANAGER: To be honest, Mrs Banks—
GLADYS: She'd be an asset. She's a hard worker. She knows all about hard work. She's honest. She's polite. She deserves a break. One little break. Are you going to be the one to offer her that break, sir?

She stares him down. He taps his fingers together for what seems like an eternity.

BANK MANAGER: Why not? [*Beat*.] Please add her name and address to this list…

He hands her a clipboard. She takes it.

… and she'll be notified of an interview time.

GLADYS *shakes her head.*

Oh! I beg your pardon.

He hands her his fountain pen. She holds it, uncertain, then hands it back. She collects her things as if to leave.

Mrs Banks? [*Beat.*] Oh, fountain pens are a little tricky, aren't they?

He calmly begins to fill out the form and GLADYS *sits back down.*

Your daughter's full name, Mrs Banks?

GLADYS: Dolores. Dolores Alice Banks.

The lights go down.

♦♦♦♦♦

SCENE ELEVEN: THE BALL

The sound of big-band swing music is heard.

When the lights come up, DOLLY *is swirling and floating around the dance floor in her full-skirted dress, with* ERROL *as her partner. She is wearing an orchid corsage.*

DOLLY: They're looking at us.
ERROL: That's 'cos you're the prettiest girl here.
DOLLY: I'm not sure…
ERROL: I am. You look a picture, Dolores. I said that.
DOLLY: You did.
ERROL: Well, you do. [*Teasing her*] And you haven't stepped on my toes once.

DOLLY *slaps him on the arm gently and he grabs the hand and squeezes it tight. The song ends but he's still holding her hand tightly.*

DOLLY: They are looking at us. Nancy Woolthorpe, and the others.
ERROL: She's probably jealous. Not to be mean, but you look much nicer than she does.

> DOLLY *is nervously pleased with his boldness.*

Now, I'll get us a punch. Don't you go anywhere, now.

> *She just giggles.* ERROL *exits to get the drinks.*
>
> *The lights change for a dream sequence.*

COMPERE: [*voice-over on a squeaky microphone*] And the winner of the Miss Mooroopna-Shepparton Ball is… Miss Dolores Banks.

> *A sash is hung over* DOLLY'*s shoulder.* DOLLY *is astounded—so excited.*
>
> *The lights snap back to reality.*

Repeating, our inaugural Miss Mooroopna-Shepparton is… Miss Nancy Woolthorpe. Could she step up, please…?

> *Clapping and cheering can be heard.*

Isn't she a picture? Put your hands together for Nancy! The prettiest little gal in town.

> *But before she accepts the sash, we hear* NANCY WOOLTHORPE'*s voice:*

NANCY: [*voice-over*] Why, if it isn't Miss Dolores Banks herself. Love your dress, Dolly. Love the fabric. [*With a giggle*] My mother quite liked it too. When it was our sunroom curtains. But, you know, I thought we took them to the tip.

> DOLLY *is frozen in shame.*

DOLLY: [*to herself*] My ball gown? Courtesy of the town bloody tip?
COMPERE: [*voice-over*] And here she is! Our very own Miss Mooroopna-Shepparton!

> DOLLY *runs out, humiliated. The band sounds die away and night sounds take over. It is dark and a weak light shines on her from the hall. Her chest is heaving as she tries to hold in the tears. From the shadows comes a voice.*

COUSIN: [*offstage, slurring*] Hey, Dolores, come over here.
DOLLY: Pardon? [*She wipes away a tear and tries to compose herself.*] I mean, what?

COUSIN: [*offstage*] Come over here, I said.
DOLLY: No.
COUSIN: [*offstage*] No? Think you're too good for us.
DOLLY: No. I don't—
COUSIN: [*offstage*] I think you do.
DOLLY: I don't—
COUSIN: [*offstage*] I reckon you need to be taught a lesson—
DOLLY: No—

> ERROL *arrives looking flustered, holding two cups of fruit punch.*

ERROL: Dolly? I've been looking all over for you. Can you believe it, that girl, in the horrible pink dress—?
COUSIN: [*offstage*] This your friend?
DOLLY: Please stop it, Leon—
COUSIN: [*offstage*] This who you step out with?
DOLLY: Leon—
ERROL: What's going on? Dolly?

> *There is a scuffle in the dark.*

DOLLY: Get your hands off me!
ERROL: Why, you don't treat a lady like that—
COUSIN: [*offstage*] She's no lady, she's just a little—

> *The big-band sound strikes up inside the hall. A drink goes flying, a punching sound, then another.* ERROL *staggers back into the weak light, holding his eye.* DOLLY *runs through the light, sobbing, her dress slightly ripped.*

[*Offstage, yelling*] See you later then, Doll—
ERROL: Dolly? Dolly?

> *But she's gone.*

◆◆◆◆◆

SCENE TWELVE: STORM BREWING

GLADYS *is knitting up a storm while* NAN *crochets.* GLADYS *looks at her watch and smiles.*

GLADYS: She'll be having a lovely time.

But NAN *has a sense of foreboding and* GLADYS *picks up on it.*
What is it?
She doesn't answer but goes outside with the kero lamp.
NAN DEAR: Dolly? Dolly?
But the only reply is the rising wind that makes the kero lamp flicker and blow out.

♦ ♦ ♦ ♦ ♦

SCENE THIRTEEN: WATERS RISING

As the lights come up, DOLLY *is sobbing down by the river. After a time she hears a noise and is startled. Again she hears a sound and raises her fists to defend herself.*

ERROL: Whoa there, Dolly. It's me.
DOLLY: I knew that'd happen.
ERROL: It wasn't very nice—
DOLLY: Nice? You heard them. It'll never change… some things never do.
ERROL: Don't say that.
DOLLY: Especially around here.
ERROL: Please.
DOLLY: It's true.
ERROL: Please, Dolly… Let's just talk, can we? Please don't run away… If I have to try and follow you again, I'll really get lost—you know about my lousy sense of direction.

He's trying to jolly her. She can't help but smile through the tears.

DOLLY: I sure do.
ERROL: Ouch.

His eye is hurting.

DOLLY: Let me look at that. You have… an ocular contusion.
ERROL: A what?
DOLLY: A black eye, buddy.

She leads him closer to the river. She reaches in and retrieves something from the river, which she places against his eye.

ERROL: What's this? Some traditional Aboriginal method?
DOLLY: It's Aeroplane jelly.
ERROL: Whatever happened to a good steak—?
DOLLY: It's mutton flaps or this.
ERROL: And you keep it in the river?
DOLLY: You see any icebox up there?
ERROL: Oh.
DOLLY: Stay still!
ERROL: Yes, Nurse Dolly.
DOLLY: Nurse… Oh. The river's rising.
ERROL: Is it? Oh… your dress!

He sees the rip in it.

DOLLY: [*with a shrug*] Who cares? It's a stupid dress.
ERROL: It's… it's the prettiest dress I've ever seen. Though you could've worn a flour bag and you would've still been the prettiest girl in the room.

Beat.

DOLLY: Really?
ERROL: Really. You're my Miss Mooroopna-Shepparton.

He moves in more intimately. Beat.

DOLLY: Really?
ERROL: Yes, really… Ouch. [*His eye is hurting.*] Say, where did you learn to hook like that?
DOLLY: Thirty big brothers. Well, three blood brothers and twenty-seven boy cousins. Who are like brothers.
ERROL: Twenty-seven cousins, whew…

DOLLY punches ERROL's arm with one knuckle.

DOLLY: Yep. That's only the boys.
ERROL: I've got three cousins that I only get to see once a year. Twenty-seven! Do you all get together at Christmas? I can't imagine how many pressies you have under the tree.

DOLLY snorts.

DOLLY: What tree? [*Pause. Wistfully*] It would be nice… to have a tree, and presents. Nancy Woolthorpe has this great big fake tree… Last year they wrapped the presents in red paper and green paper.

ERROL: Sounds like my mum. She's mad on all the trimmings. Glass baubles and fake snow…

DOLLY: I bet you have lots of presents, at your house?

ERROL: Piles! All wrapped up and tied with ribbons! With not a bow out of place. [*Beat.*] Bet you have more fun than we do, though. Your mum, your nan, your brothers, your cousins—

DOLLY: Aunties and uncles. And Papa Dear! We just have a singalong. We don't go much for presents. Except for Papa Dear. He always brings me back something special. Something from one of his trips. You know the church sent him to Western Australia?

ERROL: All that way?

DOLLY: They ask for him everywhere…! I'm talking too much…

ERROL: No, you're not… I like hearing about your life. Your family… it's different from mine. My dad expects me to call him 'sir'.

DOLLY: Gee.

ERROL: And my mum… well, she has these funny ideas sometimes… rather, my dad thinks they're funny ideas. Take this—she wants to get a job. She says she's at home, with nothing to do but bake and dust—

DOLLY: Sounds like Nancy Woolthorpe's mum.

ERROL: —but he says she's too delicate to work. Your mum chops wood! With an axe and all! And skins rabbits! It's like your family's from another country or something.

DOLLY: We are. [*Beat.*] I can look after myself, you know.

ERROL: I know that—now. And it seems you can look after me, too.

> DOLLY *giggles.*

DOLLY: But it was sweet. To come to my rescue like that.

ERROL: He called you names! Awful names!

DOLLY: He called you a gin jockey!

ERROL: [*indignant*] I told him I never touch the stuff!

> DOLLY *giggles then stops. The jelly is falling apart a little and* ERROL *eats some off his fingers.*

Port wine. Want some?

> DOLLY *starts to eat the jelly from his fingers.*

DOLLY: Port…

ERROL: … wine.

They move closer, a kiss imminent. Celestial music is heard. But then she moves away.

What's wrong, Dolly?

DOLLY: I can't.

ERROL: Why?

DOLLY: Feel like getting coshed every time we step out together? Can't walk down the street holding hands for being called names? And what would your dad say if you took me home to meet him?

ERROL is lost in thought. DOLLY moves further away from him, as if to leave.

ERROL: Dolly, I've got something to say. I want you to come away with me.

DOLLY: Away?

ERROL: Yes. To the city. We can get married. You could get a job. We can get a little flat. Wouldn't you like that? A sweet little flat with a balcony and a sitting room and a kitchen with a real stove and a new-fangled Kelvinator and water on tap… That'd have to be better than the river…

DOLLY: I'd have to leave the river…

ERROL: We could be near the seaside. Brighton's nice. It's not far from my parents…

DOLLY: I'd have to leave my family…

ERROL: Well, we could catch the train up once or twice a year. Or they could come down to visit. Though we could only afford a small flat, on my wage, so they couldn't stay over, but never mind.

DOLLY: You want me to leave here, forever?

ERROL: I'm offering you a better life.

DOLLY: A better life?

ERROL: In the city there's department stores so big you could spend all day in them. Why, in the city there's even little restaurants you can eat spaghetti, just like in Italy.

DOLLY: Spaghetti?

ERROL: The point is, you could live in a real home, for the first time.

DOLLY: A real home?

ERROL: We could even save for wall-to-wall carpet… I want to spoil you. You deserve it. You deserve better.

DOLLY: Better?

ERROL: You're repeating everything—
DOLLY: I don't understand what you're saying—
ERROL: I'm offering you a future… our future, together.
DOLLY: But… a real home? A real home is where there are people looking out for each other. [*Beat.*] Do they do that in your home, in your family, Errol?
ERROL: Well…
DOLLY: [*to herself*] Don't matter if the floors are dirt. Don't matter one bit—
ERROL: [*demanding*] Hang on. Are you saying you'd rather live in a humpy by the river? When I'm promising you the world?
DOLLY: Your world. And you're just assuming that your world is better. But actually, when I think about it—when I think about that nasty Nancy—she has everything that opens and shuts. I'm not so sure it is better. I wouldn't trade places with her for anything. And as far as what you're offering… no thank you. This is my place. I'm staying right here with my mum and my nan.
ERROL: But, Dolly—
DOLLY: No, Errol. Our life isn't perfect, but like Nan says, it's ours. And you don't respect that. I'm sorry—

> *She goes to leave but he grabs her arm. She shakes him free.*

Let go of me!
ERROL: I won't!
DOLLY: You have no right—
ERROL: Please… Dolly. I promised I'd walk you home. At least let me do that.
DOLLY: No. And don't follow me, this time. [*Beat.*] I can look after myself… remember?

> *Thunder, lightning. And she's gone into the shadows leaving him, bewildered and alone. Utterly crushed, he exits in the opposite direction. From the direction in which she's gone, we hear a sinister voice.*

COUSIN: [*offstage*] Well, hello, Dolly… thought I'd catch up with you…

> *The lights go down, then half up.*

♦ ♦ ♦ ♦ ♦

SCENE FOURTEEN: THE FLOOD

Rain and thunder and lightning.

The humpy interior is pitch-dark apart from a flickering hurricane lamp way up high on the shelf. The two women are packing up their belongings.

NAN DEAR: Grab the flour, Glad, and the tea.
GLADYS: I have done this before, Mum. [*To herself*] Only about a thousand times.

They pack up and move things higher, calmly and deliberately.

Wonder if it'll go as high as '51.
NAN DEAR: Hope not. Got too much to do. Don't want to wait three days for it to subside. [*Beat*.] Are you sure she's…?
GLADYS: Safe? He has the utility… Unless the water's already over the roads… I'm sure she'll be fine… She's sensible.
NAN DEAR: She's with a boy. That'll make her silly, not sensible.
GLADYS: [*cranky*] You want to have a go at me for letting her go with him, then come right out and say it. Don't take it out on the girl.

NAN is put out. GLADYS now focuses on the encyclopedias.

NAN DEAR: I'm worried, that's all.
GLADYS: Then just say you're worried, rather than… all that other nonsense.
NAN DEAR: I'm worried.
GLADYS: [*softer*] Mum… don't worry. I'm sure she'll be… as right as rain.

NAN tries to convince herself that she's being a worry-wart.

NAN DEAR: Yes. Right as rain.

But when there's a heavy knock at the door NAN reacts. A JUNGI (policeman) enters.

Is it my granddaughter? Is she okay?
JUNGI: Granddaughter? No, ma'am. I'm here to help you up to the tip site.
GLADYS: She was in Shepp—
JUNGI: There's no getting through tonight. They'll evacuate her to the church. If you could grab just the essentials…

NAN *struggles to lift her Singer sewing machine.*

Ma'am? Is this essential?

NAN DEAR: It's a Singer!

She plonks it in the pram.

GLADYS: Could you give us a hand with the encyclopedia set, lad?

JUNGI: My orders are to move all people first, before we move property. Property can be replaced, after all.

GLADYS: Not this, it can't. [*To herself*] Not on a picker's wage. Gawd, we'd be living on Johnny cakes. [*Pleading*] Look, it's real important. For my daughter, see. Not for me, but for my daughter. Please.

JUNGI: Rightio… Now if you would just—

GLADYS: You'll make sure they're high and dry?

JUNGI: Yes. Let's get on with it.

GLADYS hoists the bag of food over her shoulder and rushes up to help NAN with the pram. The JUNGI shepherds them out of the humpy. A noise outside makes GLADYS alert.

GLADYS: It's a banshee wailing.

Suddenly, a flash of lightning illuminates the statue-like figure of DOLLY. The sight of her makes GLADYS freeze, as if she's seen a ghost. But NAN runs towards her.

The second verse of 'Que Sera, Sera' can be heard: 'Then I grew up and fell in love…'

DOLLY pushes NAN aside and resolutely steps towards the humpy. But when she reaches the door the JUNGI puts his hand up.

JUNGI: You can't go in there. We're evacuating.

DOLLY is looking down, shamefully, but still she defies him and goes to push past. He is astounded that someone would defy him and reaches to grab her arm. She half screams.

DOLLY: [*low*] Don't touch me.

She steps inside the humpy.

GLADYS: [*panicking*] There's another family. Down here. With six children. [*She points.*] Help them.

The JUNGI shrugs and starts to move off. NAN follows GLADYS back into the humpy. The JUNGI, looking around for somewhere to put the crate containing the encyclopedias, places them on the ground. He vanishes into the dark.

The song continues: 'I asked my sweetheart, what lies ahead...'

Inside the humpy GLADYS *and* NAN *whisper in private.* GLADYS *then approaches* DOLLY.

Dolly, what is it? Dolly, please?

DOLLY *ignores them.* GLADYS *stands there helpless.*

Oh, my God. What has happened to you?

She wails like a banshee.

Rain, thunder, darkness.

Time passes.

The waters rise.

END OF ACT ONE

ACT TWO

SCENE ONE: AFTER THE FLOOD

Dawn finds GLADYS *outside the humpy. The water has drained away, but the devastation has been wrought. Everything is saturated and muddy.* GLADYS *is agitated.* NAN *leads* DOLLY *out onto a kero-tin seat that catches a ray of sunshine. She's still in the same dress, badly ripped and muddied. She's shell-shocked.* NAN *hands her a cup of billy tea.*

NAN DEAR: That was a bit of a struggle.

>GLADYS *looks anxious.*

To find dry wood.

GLADYS: And clean water.

>*They are trying to be light, but their hearts are heavy.*

NAN DEAR: At least the tea was dry, eh, Dolly?

>*But she doesn't answer.* GLADYS *has discovered the box of encyclopedias and she's distracted, so she hasn't listened to the others.* NAN *hands* GLADYS *a cup of tea.*

GLADYS: Least the tea was dry, eh?

>NAN *notices the encyclopedias.*

NAN DEAR: Oh, my… oh, Gladys…

>DOLLY *doesn't even register.*

Every one, Gladys? Every single one, ruined?

GLADYS: Never mind.

NAN DEAR: Never mind! They were your dream—

GLADYS: [*fiercely*] No! No! They're only possessions. And what do they matter? People is what matters.

>*They both look at* DOLLY. *Beat.*

NAN DEAR: I've been thinking… Gladys… If you still want to move to Rumbalara… It'd be better for the girl…

GLADYS: [*by rote*] She's not a girl.

They both know it.

[*Whispering to* NAN] Should we send word to Papa Dear?
NAN DEAR: [*whispering back*] I think… best not. It's women's business.

They look at each other in despair, barely able to hold it together. Just then ERROL *appears with a determined look on his face.*

ERROL: Dolly, I'm sorry. I've come to beg your [*forgiveness*]—
NAN DEAR: You've got a cheek. Showing your face—
GLADYS: You're responsible? You did this?
ERROL: What? [*He looks at her dishevelled state.*] Oh, my—Dolly, what happened—?
NAN DEAR: You get the hell—!
GLADYS: [*angrily*] Please leave. Now!
ERROL: But, Nan Dear, Gladys—
NAN DEAR: Don't you ever dare call me that—
ERROL: I would never—
GLADYS: Are you leaving? Or do I have to—?

GLADYS *reaches for the axe.* ERROL *stops and backs off.*

ERROL: [*devastated*] I thought you knew me.
GLADYS: I thought I did too.

The two women move to stand by DOLLY's *side, in unity. Devastated,* ERROL *turns and leaves. They watch him depart, still angry.*

NAN DEAR: If he ever shows his face—
DOLLY: It wasn't him.

DOLLY *goes inside the humpy. The two women look at each other in shock.*

The lights down, then up to the sound of bulldozers.

♦ ♦ ♦ ♦ ♦

SCENE TWO: THE MOVE TO RUMBALARA

RADIO: [*voice-over*] From riverbank humpy to white house is quite a step. It will shortly become reality for the Aboriginal residents of the tin and canvas shanties. The ready-made concrete sections are rapidly being fitted into place. The neat, new, prefabricated house is the first nearly completed unit in a new group of ten. This is the most vigorous attempt yet to solve Aboriginal housing...

> NAN *and* GLADYS *hold their humble possessions as the sound of the bulldozers is heard. Their humpy disappears.*

GLADYS: It'll be wonderful, you'll see. Dolly'll love it. Just love it.

> *The sound of construction.*

> NAN *starts to cough (and coughs whenever she is in the house from now on).*

> *The lights go down, then come up on the new housing. It's concrete, small, white and featureless. It's anything but lovable.*

NAN DEAR: Not quite the 'new deal'.
GLADYS: No.
NAN DEAR: [*grimly*] I'll make curtains.
GLADYS: Yes, Mum. Thank you.

> *The lights go down.*

♦ ♦ ♦ ♦ ♦

SCENE THREE: THE BROADCAST

The lights come up on DOLLY *who is peeling big dirty potatoes.*

RADIO: [*voice-over*] It's Australia's Amateur Hour... where we showcase Australia's most talented performers. Here's one of them now...

> *We hear a man playing a gumleaf.*

> GLADYS *enters and looks around conspiratorially.*

GLADYS: Nan's out? This came for you.

> *She holds a letter. No response from* DOLLY.

Aren't you going to read it? It's from the bank.
DOLLY: If you know so much, you read it.
GLADYS: It's an opportunity.
DOLLY: It's an interview for a job I'm not going to get. And that you want, not me. [*To herself*] Why doesn't anyone ask what I want?

> *She flicks the station in frustration.*

RADIO: [*voice-over*] … the historic broadcast of the Rodney Shire Council meeting. On the agenda is Aboriginal housing…

GLADYS is momentarily distracted by the radio.

GLADYS: Housing? [*To* DOLLY, *frustrated*] So you're just going to give up?

DOLLY: Yes.

GLADYS: Dolly, please—

DOLLY: [*bitter*] Look at you, Mum. You go on about the things I should be doing. Why don't you fix your own house? If you know what I mean…

GLADYS looks at her, and something snaps.

GLADYS: Well! I'll show you!

NAN enters, drawn by the raised voices.

NAN DEAR: What's going on?

GLADYS picks up her hat and handbag.

Where you going now?

GLADYS: To fix my own house.

GLADYS exits in a determined fashion.

NAN DEAR: What?

A bicycle bell rings violently. NAN *looks out the window.*

She's got a bee in her bonnet about something. [*She turns to* DOLLY *suspiciously.*] What were you arguing about?

DOLLY: She wants me to go for that bank job.

NAN DEAR: You told her that's silly?

DOLLY: Of course. How will I ever get a job now?

NAN *just looks at her thoughtfully. There's a knock on the door.* NAN *marches up to the door, grabbing a jam tin on the way. She opens the door and the* RENT COLLECTOR *is standing there.*

NAN DEAR: Mr Coody.

RENT COLLECTOR: Mrs Dear.

Silently she hands him the money. He slowly and deliberately counts each coin, writes out a receipt and hands it to her. She takes the receipt and moves back inside. She joins DOLLY *and begins shelling peas into some newspaper as if nothing has happened.*

They work in companionable silence, NAN *occasionally stopping to read the paper.*

NAN DEAR: Do you read this here page for children? It's called the Piccaninny's Page... Fancy calling it that?

    DOLLY *shakes her head.* NAN *continues to read the paper.*

Says they've got this new powder that's 'guaranteed to turn your skin white'. Know a few folk who'd like to get their hands on that!

DOLLY: Nan, you never sit down and read.

NAN DEAR: [*whispering*] I can't in front of her.

DOLLY: [*whispering back*] She's not here [*loudly*] so just go and read it. For once. Gosh, Nan.

    DOLLY *shoos her to the seat with the paper.* DOLLY *takes over shelling the peas. The music ends on the radio.*

RADIO ANNOUNCER: [*voice-over*] We resume our live broadcast of the Rodney Shire Council meeting...

COUNCILLOR 1: [*voice-over*] ...on Crown Land. We bulldozed the shanties but they're creeping back. This housing problem is not going away. The lack of sanitation poses a serious risk to the good people of our town—

NAN DEAR: This rubbish!

    NAN *walks over to the radio...*

COUNCILLOR 2: [*voice-over*] Why can't an ablutions block be built out there?

    ... to turn it off, but just before she does she hears:

GLADYS: [*voice-over*] Excuse me...

    NAN *stares at the radio.*

NAN DEAR: That's her.

DOLLY: What?

NAN DEAR: Shh!

COUNCILLOR 1: [*voice-over*] The night cart, for one, can't get access for part of the year due to the flooding—

GLADYS: [*voice-over*] If I could say something...

NAN DEAR: See!

    She points to the radio.

COUNCILLOR 2: [*voice-over*] Then build it at Daish's Paddock.

COUNCILLOR 1: [*voice-over*] That's out of the question.
GLADYS: [*voice-over*] Why so?
COUNCILLOR 1: [*voice-over*] Daish's is our town tip site, that serves the whole of our community, not just an itinerant minority, as the councillor for the West Ward well knows…

There's a roar from outraged councillors.

GLADYS: [*voice-over*] Oi! Re the so-called 'housing problem', it is a housing problem because us Aboriginals—

NAN and DOLLY are getting very excited.

CHAIRMAN: [*voice-over*] Madam…
DOLLY: They're calling her madam!
NAN DEAR: Shh!
GLADYS: [*voice-over*] —us Aboriginals are not welcome in the townships—
CHAIRMAN: [*voice-over*] Madam!

GLADYS needs to fight to be heard over the roars of the councillors.

GLADYS: [*voice-over*] And apart from those concrete humpies that you built—call them houses?
CHAIRMAN: [*voice-over*] Order! I must insist—
GLADYS: [*voice-over*] And what about the other families? If you won't let us build our own houses on higher ground—
CHAIRMAN: [*voice-over*] The Chair does not recognise this—
GLADYS: [*voice-over*] —as if we choose to live on a floodplain—not realising that we need water too—to cook and to clean—
DOLLY: Go, Mum!
CHAIRMAN: [*voice-over*] There are protocols! If you read the rules—
GLADYS: [*voice-over*] Maybe you don't think we do wash—
CHAIRMAN: [*voice-over*] Eject this interloper—
GLADYS: [*voice-over*] I'm not an interloper—I belong here—this is my land!
CHAIRMAN: [*voice-over*] Madam, read the rules! Eject her!
CROWD: [*voice-over*] Hear! Hear!
GLADYS: [*voice-over*] I haven't finished. In fact I'm just starting re 'the housing problem'…

Her voice fades out as she is being led away.

NAN *picks up the radio and shakes it.*

NAN DEAR: Oh… schizenhausen!

DOLLY: What?

NAN DEAR: The bloody valve!

    DOLLY *is flabbergasted.*

Oh, don't look at me like that! As if you've never heard someone swear.

DOLLY: In German?

    NAN *shakes it off.*

NAN DEAR: But my daughter. My Gladys! Did you hear her?

    She's practically hugging the radio, as if it were GLADYS.

I didn't think you had it in you, daught. [*To* DOLLY] Did you?

DOLLY: Not really.

    They dance a little jig around the radio as the lights fade.

SCENE FOUR: THE CONTRACT

ERROL *hurries up the track and is relieved to see* GLADYS—*in a similar scene to the first time he saw her, chopping wood—but this time outside the new Rumbalara housing.* ERROL *approaches her very tentatively.*

ERROL: Mrs Banks?

    GLADYS *turns around.*

GLADYS: Errol?

ERROL: Can I…?

    He means 'approach'. She nods and when she puts down the axe he feels able to step forward.

You're here now?

GLADYS: Yes.

ERROL: Took a bit to find you—

GLADYS: Why are you here, Errol?

ERROL: I'm sorry to bother you. It's about the—

GLADYS & ERROL: [*simultaneously*] Encyclopedias.

GLADYS: We… I… won't be needing them anymore. All the shillings go into the meter box now.

ERROL: Isn't there any way…?
GLADYS: No.
ERROL: Oh… Thing is, the contract. You signed it.
GLADYS: Yes.
ERROL: So you need to cancel it. You're not meant to be able to. But there are circumstances…
GLADYS: I have 'circumstances' all right.
ERROL: But it has to be done in writing.
GLADYS: Well, I can't, can I? [*Beat.*] I can't.
ERROL: You mean, you can't write?
GLADYS: You're slow on the uptake, lad.
ERROL: I've never met anyone—
GLADYS: —that can't read and write?
ERROL: Yes.
GLADYS: Now you have.
ERROL: It's none of my business, Mrs Banks, but you're a smart lady.

Beat.

GLADYS: I'm sorry about last time, Errol. I wasn't so smart then. I treated you unfairly…
ERROL: I still don't understand… Dolly was so upset… I wished she could have heard me out…

Beat.

GLADYS: Thing is, I'm sorry.
ERROL: Thank you, Mrs Banks.

They're both awkward. He holds out his hand to shake on it.

Thing is, ma'am, the letter…
GLADYS: The letter.
ERROL: We still need to write this letter.
GLADYS: We?
ERROL: We.

So she nods and they both sit down on the kero tins. Resting a piece of paper on ERROL's *book, they start to compose a letter together,* ERROL *writing it down.*

The song 'Catch a Falling Star' plays in the background.

GLADYS: Are you still up this way frequent, like?

ERROL: Still got half the alphabet to deliver.
GLADYS: Could I ask you a favour, Errol? I can't ask my mother—she works day and night. And Dolly's offered, but—
ERROL: How is Dolly?
GLADYS: She's… she's okay.
ERROL: Do you think she'd—?
GLADYS: No, Errol, she won't see you. I'm sure of that.

A beat while they think about DOLLY, *each with their own sorrows and regrets.*

ERROL: The favour?
GLADYS: Could you teach me, Errol? See, we had a school and good teachers at Cummeragunja at one time, that's why Mum has such beautiful handwriting, but then the mission managers were terrible and it was all downhill, and I got sent off to work for a family. A family of six and a big house to look after—who had time for learning? Then I married Len and we were picking and along came the children, and then the war, and we were all so busy knitting for the war effort and I thought I'd get around to learning from someone but they were all… so busy.
ERROL: I had no idea… that any of that went on…
GLADYS: Then my darn pride got in the way—
ERROL: It'd be an honour, Mrs Banks.
GLADYS: It would…? Thank you.
ERROL: Pleasure. [*Beat.*] So she's—
GLADYS: She's changed. I am sorry, Errol.
ERROL: Then I'll have to change too. I'll prove to her I can. That I'm worthy of her.

He gets up, folds the letter into the envelope and licks it.

GLADYS: You do that, Errol. You just do that.

The lights go down.

♦ ♦ ♦ ♦ ♦

SCENE FIVE: PAY THE RENT

Time passes.

The song 'Somewhere Over the Rainbow' plays.

As the lights come up, it is early morning, but already blindingly hot.
NAN is cooking outside, just like she used to.

DOLLY: [*offstage*] Morning, Nan.
NAN DEAR: One egg or two, Dolly love?
DOLLY: [*offstage*] How'd you know I felt like eggs? Three.
NAN DEAR: A serve of eggs is just what you need—

The RENT COLLECTOR *is standing there.*

Mr Coody.
RENT COLLECTOR: Mrs Dear.
DOLLY: [*offstage*] Gawd, Nan, it's only just past seven and already it's stinking hot. Tonight I'll have to sleep on the roof like the others. Imagine me clambering up there—

She walks in, heavily pregnant, and stops dead when she sees the RENT COLLECTOR *who looks with disdain at her body.*

RENT COLLECTOR: Your arrangements will need to be re-evaluated, with the impending new arrival. I'm not sure that the house is suitable for an extended family—
NAN DEAR: That's not of your concern.

She gets the eggs out of the basket.

RENT COLLECTOR: It is very much of my concern. Everything to do with the habitation of this establishment is my concern.
NAN DEAR: This is Aboriginal Housing… [*under her breath*] not your own private kingdom.

DOLLY *makes a sharp moan.*

Go in, Doll.

NAN *passes over the rent book and the payment.*

Here's the rent. Please leave.
RENT COLLECTOR: And the person I saw just leaving?
NAN DEAR: The midwife.
RENT COLLECTOR: I should think the hospital is a more suitable place—
NAN DEAR: [*to herself*] And hospitals is where they take our babies away.
RENT COLLECTOR: You realise it is outside visiting hours? Given your obvious flouting of the rules, I think—

NAN DEAR: I don't care what you think! You and your visiting hours. Your rules. No singalongs after dark. Your spying. You, mister, can go to blazes! I'll give you 'one'…

She raises an egg as he turns.

Two… Oh hell, three.

He runs. NAN *chucks the eggs, one after the other, at his departing form.*

DOLLY: Nan! What would Papa Dear say?!

NAN DEAR: Well, Papa Dear is not here to hear, is he?

DOLLY *gives* NAN *a hug.*

And sorry, love, just run out of eggs.

DOLLY: Not sure I felt like 'em anyway.

DOLLY *looks vulnerable, sad.* NAN *looks away to hide her upset. She notices* DOLLY*'s school assignment, the family tree, pinned up on the wall above them.* DOLLY *follows* NAN*'s glance.*

I never did get to finish that. Now there'll be a new name to add to it. I was thinking Reg, or if it's a girl… Regina. What do you think?

NAN DEAR: After Papa Dear? He'll be thrilled.

DOLLY: Nan, there's something I need to tell you… about that night—

NAN DEAR: Hush…

Beat.

DOLLY: But I'm worried —that I won't love it. Because of—

NAN DEAR: No matter how they come into the world, you still love 'em the same.

DOLLY: Even if—

NAN DEAR: Even if.

DOLLY: Nan. About that night, at the cork trees—

NAN DEAR: You don't need to say a thing. I was your age once, too. And I even became a mother too, when I was your age. Now that you're a woman, I can tell you.

DOLLY *smiles—she's finally a woman in* NAN*'s eyes. But her smile is tinged with sadness.*

There was this lad—my father had given him some work splitting posts—work was scarce. So on this particular day, it was the day the

Great War had been declared, and he was full of fightin' spirit—and the other kind, that comes in a flagon—this lad, I knew him, and I, well, I liked him, and I thought… At seventeen you have these silly dreams, even if he was a whitefella—

DOLLY: What? A whitefella?

NAN DEAR: Yes. [*Beat.*] What I'm trying to say is… that I married Papa Dear after I was pregnant with Gladys.

DOLLY: [*not comprehending*] That's all right, Nan—you were just married in the bush way. Even if Papa Dear was a preacher.

NAN DEAR: No, Dolly—See, I was walking home, taking a short cut, and—and—and the lad—he took advantage of me…

DOLLY: What are you saying, Nan? Oh, Nan. Oh, Nan… not you…

NAN: Yes.

DOLLY: Not you, too, Nan.

NAN nods and they hold each other.

NAN DEAR: And that's why I didn't want you to have anything to do with—

DOLLY: A white boy?

NAN DEAR: Yes.

DOLLY: But it wasn't a… [*white boy*]

NAN DEAR: I realise that… now.

DOLLY: And Errol would never do anything like that.

NAN DEAR: You were so angry with him.

DOLLY: He wanted to take me away. He didn't understand that I could never leave you. He thought he was some kind of knight in shining armour. And he wasn't.

Beat.

NAN DEAR: Sometimes, you have to move on. Leave things behind… Even things you love.

Beat.

DOLLY: [*softly*] He said he wanted to marry me.

NAN DEAR: You can't marry him.

DOLLY: I hardly think he'd marry me now—

NAN DEAR: Because the lad, on the day war was declared, his name was—

DOLLY: What does that matter now? That was then—

NAN DEAR: —his name was Clem Fisher.

DOLLY: Fisher?
NAN DEAR: Yes.
DOLLY: And Errol's a Fisher.
NAN DEAR: Yes.
DOLLY: And they could be… related? Ah… I see.

Now it's NAN*'s turn to be anxious.*

NAN DEAR: I know you like that boy—
DOLLY: Oh, no, Nan. I mean, yes. But, no.

DOLLY *shakes her head. She knows it's impossible.*

NAN DEAR: More than like him? Maybe you even love him? Do you?
DOLLY: Nan, I'll respect you. I will. I promise.
NAN DEAR: I'm sorry.
DOLLY: Finito. That's it then. Que sera, sera. [*Beat.*] Please don't tell Mum about the cork trees.
NAN DEAR: She has her suspicions.
DOLLY: Please.

NAN *nods.*

NAN DEAR. And you won't…?
DOLLY: Tell Mum? About Papa Dear? No.
NAN DEAR: Us Dears and our secrets, eh?
DOLLY: Yes. [*Beat.*] Where is Mum?
NAN DEAR: Extra shift.
DOLLY: What's she saving for this time?
NAN DEAR: A lemon layette from Trevaks.
DOLLY: But she could knit one.
NAN DEAR: You know Gladys, nothing like a bought one.

They laugh. DOLLY *strokes her tummy.*

DOLLY: Perhaps you're right, Nan… I feel I could love it…
NAN DEAR: Don't you know by now that I'm right about everything!

They both laugh.

Everything'll be fine. You'll see.
DOLLY: Yes, Nan. Yes, Nan.

DOLLY *leans against* NAN *and closes her eyes.*

The lights go down.

◆ ◆ ◆ ◆ ◆

SCENE SIX: ERROL SPILLS THE BEANS

The lights come up on GLADYS *and* ERROL, *sitting on a park bench, with the Inspector's report.*

GLADYS: Anyway, I tried to say my bit at the Council meeting—
ERROL: That must have been something!
GLADYS: Well… it achieved nothing… Now everyone is cranky with me… The families for drawing attention to us… people in the street… even Papa Dear had heard about my 'radio moment'.

She sighs. Beat.

ERROL: Oh! Mrs Banks, if you're interested, we have a bonus volume—

He passes her an encyclopedia.

GLADYS: No, Errol. Thank you, but no.

He puts the book away.

ERROL: That's okay, Mrs Banks.
GLADYS: Aunty… Anyway, I sure appreciate you taking the time, Errol.
ERROL: Don't mention it, Mrs—Aunty. You sure you wouldn't like to try something…?
GLADYS: Easier? No. We'll continue with this. I'm interested to hear what he has to say about us… [*Reading, hesitatingly*] 'During September I visited with thirty families who were in permanent res…'
ERROL: Residence.
GLADYS: '… residence, some at the site of the town tip, known as Daish's Paddock, but most on the banks of the Gool…'
ERROL: Goulburn.
GLADYS: Of course. 'Goulburn River. The san—it—ta—sanitation arrangements were as follows…' [*She shakes her head and closes the report.*] I'll continue with that later.
ERROL: You're coming along nicely.
GLADYS: I get nervous in front of people. [*Beat.*] Speaking of people… how is your family?

His face clouds over.

ERROL: My family? Same as always, I guess. And yours?

GLADYS: Nan Dear, she has these little turns sometimes. Doesn't like the new housing one bit. Can't say I blame her. Won't go to the doctor, of course. My father, Reginald Dear, is still preaching. I don't know where he gets the strength.

ERROL: I'd like to meet him one day.

GLADYS: You would?

ERROL: Yes. One day. [*Pause.*] And how is…?

GLADYS: Dolly?

He nods.

She's…

ERROL: She's…?

GLADYS: Errol, straight up, what are your feelings towards the girl?

ERROL: Well, I think she's real—

GLADYS: Pretty?

ERROL: Very pretty—she's a living doll—but she's also—

GLADYS: Clever.

ERROL: Clever? She's sharp as a tack. And she's—

GLADYS: Kind.

ERROL: Kind as, but in a way that's very—

GLADYS: Modest.

ERROL: Yes, modest. She doesn't have tickets on herself. I like that about her. And I really like that fact that Dolly is—

GLADYS: Straightforward. Tells you what she wants.

Beat.

ERROL: No. She's not. I'm never sure what she wants.

GLADYS: But that can't be! She's always blurting out things, she can't help it. She's a Dear, and us Dears are well known for being straight talkers. I always talk plain—and her grandfather, Papa Dear—why, not a more straight-talking man ever walked God's earth than my dear dad.

ERROL: Your 'dear' dad.

GLADYS: He is a dear—not just because he's my dad, but because of all the things he does to help our people. [*Beat.*] There is a public meeting, in Melbourne next week. He's raising the housing issue once again. Would you like to come along? And meet him?

ERROL: I'd like that.

GLADYS: Of course Dolly'll be there. Maybe you can talk. You know what I mean—far be it from me to put words in your mouth! And, Errol…?
ERROL: Yes, Gladys?
GLADYS: Whatever she thinks, I think you're beaut.
ERROL: I think you're beaut, too.

He goes to shake hands with her, but she pulls him into a hug.

GLADYS: Thanks for spelling out your feelings towards the girl.
ERROL: That's okay. I even like her snotty googles. She's—
GLADYS: Special. She is. I couldn't have put it better myself!

The lights go down.

◆ ◆ ◆ ◆ ◆

SCENE SEVEN: THE PETITION

The lights come up on the interior of a draughty hall with the impression of rows of seats. The three women, in their Sunday best, are sitting facing the audience on a row of seats.

A finger tapping on a microphone can be heard over a loudspeaker accompanied by the squeal of feedback.

MAN ON MICROPHONE: [*voice-over*] Ladies and gentlemen, distinguished guests…
GLADYS: This is a big moment for Aboriginal people.
MAN ON MICROPHONE: [*voice-over, microphone*] This is a big moment for Aboriginal people…

The women laugh.

DOLLY: [*whispering*] You should be up there making the speech, Mum.
NAN DEAR: Gawd no, that's men's business.
DOLLY: Not always, Nan. What's women's business, anyway?
NAN DEAR: Family business, that's what.
DOLLY: [*whispering*] Keeping the secrets, you mean. [*To* GLADYS] I'm sorry, Mum, about the bank interview.
GLADYS: [*whispering*] Well, why didn't you tell me about the nursing? My girl, a nurse! On a scholarship and all!

DOLLY: There was nothing in writing. I couldn't.
GLADYS: Keeping secrets from your own mother! Fancy—you going all the way to Melbourne. You sure that's what you want?
DOLLY: I'm sure, Mum. And with Nan's help with Regina…

They both look at the pram and smile. ERROL *walks in and makes his way over to* GLADYS *who hasn't seen him yet.*

NAN DEAR: [*pushing her lips in* ERROL's *direction*] What's he doing here?
GLADYS: I invited him.

GLADYS *welcomes* ERROL. *He sits down between her and* DOLLY *and peeks in the pram.*

ERROL: Hello, Dolly.

DOLLY *looks down.* GLADYS *jumps into action.*

GLADYS: Come on, Mum, let's keep an eye out for Papa Dear.
NAN DEAR: But…
GLADYS: Mum… Papa Dear'll want to see you…

She practically drags a reluctant NAN *away, leaving* DOLLY *and* ERROL *alone.*

ERROL: Your cousin's baby?

DOLLY *isn't sure how to answer.*

'Course not. That was a little boy.

DOLLY *arranges the blankets in the pram tenderly.* ERROL *looks searchingly at* DOLLY.

She's not…
DOLLY: [*nodding*] She is.
ERROL: Why didn't you tell me? Why didn't anyone tell me?
DOLLY: It's not your business.
ERROL: [*stiffly*] You're married then. Congratulations.
DOLLY: No need.

He looks at her hand. No ring. He thinks hard.

ERROL: Nine, ten months ago. That would've been around—
DOLLY: Please—
ERROL: The flood. That's why—
DOLLY: Please.

ERROL: I'm so slow on the uptake. Damn. I'm an idiot. Damn. [*Beat.*] Are you okay?

DOLLY: Yes. I'm okay.

ERROL: Are you sure? Is there anything I can do? Of course not—you can look after yourself.

DOLLY: Most of the time.

ERROL: Dolly, I'm sorry. For everything.

DOLLY: Yes. Me too.

MAN ON MICROPHONE: [*voice-over*] We're just waiting on Papa Dear to present this here petition to you all.

VOICE FROM THE CROWD: [*offstage*] Been waiting years!

> *Laughter from offstage.*

ERROL: I had hoped we could talk. About the future.

DOLLY: The future's different now.

ERROL: Yes, it is… I've changed, Dolly. I realise I was wrong. For example, I will come up here, if you want. Because, where you belong, and your family, is important. To you, and to me.

DOLLY: I'm going to Melbourne. To nurse.

ERROL: You are? That's… great. Good on you. Nurse Dolly… [*Beat.*] Dolly…

DOLLY: Yes?

ERROL: Do you know what's in my heart?

DOLLY: Yes.

> *He searches her face but she is looking in the direction of* NAN *who is returning in a purposeful manner,* GLADYS *making up the rear.*

I'm sorry… as much as I… I just can't… I can't explain… but I can't do… this.

> *She means her and him.*

ERROL: Are you sure? Really sure?

> *She nods.*

Then I'll respect your decision…

> *But the longing between them is palpable. He turns away from them.*

And I wish you all the happiness in the world. You, and your lovely little daughter. And I hope we can at least be friends.

DOLLY: I'd… like that.

ERROL turns away from her, to hide his emotions. NAN, *now beside* DOLLY, *suddenly looks faint.*

NAN DEAR: Oh… I think it's too much for me.

She means Papa Dear's occasion. She sits down with a thud.

A glass of lemonade.

GLADYS: Quick, Dolly, go.

DOLLY *jumps up to do as she's asked.*

NAN DEAR: No, I need her.

GLADYS: Okay, Mum.

She hurries away. NAN *gestures for* DOLLY *to come closer. In the background we hear the assembly singing 'The Old Rugged Cross' very faintly.* DOLLY *looks at* NAN *expectantly, but* NAN *is unusually nervous.*

NAN DEAR: I need a powder.

DOLLY: [*sternly*] You're not pulling tricks on me?

NAN DEAR: No.

Realising it's serious, DOLLY *goes to leave, but* NAN *grabs her arm.*

Dolly—that lad.

DOLLY: I told him, Nan. I told him we can never be together. [*Beat.*] I'll go get the Bex… Will you be okay here with Errol, Nan, 'til I get back?

NAN DEAR: 'Spose. No way I'm going to fall off my perch in his company.

DOLLY *steps away.* ERROL *steps up to* NAN.

ERROL: If you want, Mrs Dear, I could drive you to the hospital.

NAN DEAR: No hospitals. That's where you go to die.

ERROL: Perhaps you'd like to go home? The company utility's outside.

NAN DEAR: You'd do that? Drive an old woman home? To Mooroopna?

ERROL: Of course. Even to the river. The Murray—that's your place, isn't it?

NAN DEAR: [*staring at him*] Brought up to respect your elders, eh?

ERROL: Yes—just like Dolly.

NAN's moved, but tries to hide it with gruffness.

NAN DEAR: Fisher? What kind of fool name is that for someone who couldn't even gut a fish?

ERROL: I've never even caught a fish.

NAN DEAR: Thought not, your hands are too soft. What kind of man has soft hands?

DOLLY returns with a packet of Bex and a glass of water, but hangs back, curious. It's the first time she's seen NAN speak directly to ERROL.

ERROL: Actually, ma'am, my dad changed our surname after the war. After they emigrated here. It was originally Vischer. But we Germans weren't the most popular. People used to throw stones at our house.

NAN DEAR: Oh? They did? [*She almost seems happy to hear this. It dawns on her.*] So you're a fake Fisher?

ERROL: 'Fraid so.

NAN DEAR: Not even a real one?

ERROL: 'Fraid not.

NAN DEAR: Not related to any Fishers, even?

ERROL: No, ma'am.

It dawns on DOLLY and NAN simultaneously.

DOLLY: That means…

NAN DEAR: Dear God. Thank goodness.

NAN reaches over and gives him a smacking kiss on the cheek. DOLLY stands there, agape. GLADYS rushes up with the glass of lemonade—she hasn't seen the kiss.

GLADYS: Here's your lemonade, Mum.

NAN DEAR: You know I never touch that stuff. Bad for my sugars. Give it to Dolly.

GLADYS is completely exasperated. She has not yet noticed DOLLY's expression.

WOMAN ON MICROPHONE: [*voice-over*] We can't wait much longer for your father.

GLADYS: He'll be here.

WOMAN ON MICROPHONE: [*voice-over*] Right you are…

DOLLY's baby cries and GLADYS *turns her attention to the pram. She's speaking to* DOLLY, *not even noticing the* DOLLY *and* NAN's *sudden mood change.* ERROL *is just bewildered.*

GLADYS: Papa Dear will be here soon. I hope that you, Regina, will be as lucky as I am. Papa Dear… he's the best father a girl could ever have.

DOLLY: [*to* GLADYS] Mum, I've got something to tell you. Papa Dear's not—

The squeal of a microphone.

GLADYS: Not what? Not coming? 'Course he is!

DOLLY *hesitates.*

WOMAN ON MICROPHONE: [*voice-over*] Ah… we've just had word. Papa Dear's been caught up at a funeral. If Uncle Wally is here, can he present the petition? Where are you, Uncle?

GLADYS *stares in the direction of the voice, then something snaps.*

GLADYS: Petition. Uncle Wally… What's he got to do with this?

She marches up to the podium.

I will present the petition. [*Tremulous*] After all, me and my father Papa Dear, we came up with this here petition together… Gawd, I'm nervous— [*To an audience member*] Oh, hi there, Aunty…

She closes her eyes and without looking at the paper she begins.

As you know, William Cooper tried to present a petition to King George a few years back, but it was refused. Maybe our current monarch will listen to what we have to say.

Her Majesty, Queen Elizabeth the Second, Queen of England and her territories. We humbly present this petition to you… [*To herself*] Why humbly? We've been humble too long. Anyway… [*She continues confidently.*] We request… [*To herself*] No, we don't, sorry Papa. [*Continuing*] We demand to be heard.

CROWD: [*offstage*] Hear, hear.

GLADYS: Your Majesty, Queen Elizabeth the Second. We demand suitable housing for the Aboriginal people. [*To herself*] Yes, we got Rumbalara. And I'll be the first to admit, the idea sounded good. But—have you seen it? Concrete. No doors inside—so, we don't need privacy, not like regular folk, is that it? We want decent houses. Mrs Windsor, would you live at Rumbalara? Then why is it good enough for us? Why do we have to prove we can live like whitefellas, before we get the same opportunities? And, to boot, we're watched over like a bunch of cheeky kids... We're second-class citizens in our own country. No, we're not even citizens. Heavens, and this is the fifties!

We demand the right to control our own destiny. Now how exactly did Papa Dear word it...?

She looks at the paper. She's lost her train of thought. She begins to panic. She's up in public, reading. She looks at the piece of paper wildly.

VOICE: [*offstage*] Do you need your glasses?
GLADYS: No.

There is a sustained moment of tension, then she hesitatingly reads one word, then another, then another.

'We demand the right to make our own decisions, and not be at the whim of government, at the mercy of Protection Boards, at the vagary of landlords and property owners.'

'We demand proper schooling.' [*To herself*] And not just for us. [*Continuing*] 'The white people too—they need to be educated about us, and our ways.'

She is reading more fluently now.

'Opportunities. We want jobs in town for our sons and daughters. We want them to go to universities.' [*To herself*] Yes! Not just high schools but universities! And why not? They say we can't learn, but we can. We can do anything once we set our minds to it, eh?

'We, the undersigned, demand to be the equal of anyone. And we will fight for that right. And keep fighting. Until we are treated right. By our neighbours and employers. By the Shire, by the Crown, by Mr Menzies.' [*To herself*] And if it's not him, then the next Prime Minister. Or the one after that.

Lastly, and this isn't in the petition, but maybe it should be, I don't want my mother to be served last in the butcher's. And I want townsfolk to say, 'Hello, lovely day'. Not cross the road to avoid us like we're lepers. [*To her audience*] We can get along with each other, can't we?

> ERROL *and* DOLLY *look at each other, longingly.* NAN, *as always, notices this and smiles.* GLADYS *has revved the crowd into a frenzy, but as she looks at them, she stops abruptly, her natural modesty reasserting itself.*

Goodness, I think I've said more than enough. But please, sign our petition. Come up to me afterwards. If you want me to read any part to you… I can. Thank you.

> GLADYS *ends her speech to tumultuous applause.* DOLLY *and* ERROL *again look at each other, very emotionally, clapping hard.*

VOICE: [*offstage, yelling*] That's the spirit. She's Papa Dear's daughter all right!

> GLADYS *joins her family, excitedly. They hug her.*

NAN DEAR: You done us all proud, Gladys. Your dad'd be…

> *A knowing look passes between* NAN *and* DOLLY.

… real proud of ya.

> *The baby makes a sound, as if she wants some of this attention.* ERROL *and* DOLLY *both automatically turn to the pram.*
>
> *The last verse of 'Que Sera, Sera' begins:*
>
>> 'Now I have children of my own…'
>
> *The lights change for* NAN'*s dream sequence.*
>
> *Wedding bells and confetti as* DOLLY *and* ERROL—*pram in the middle—get hitched.*
>
> *The lights snap back to reality:*
>
>> 'They asked their mother, what will I be…'

NAN DEAR: Oh, for heaven's sake! Dolly, marry this boy, before someone else does—I saw your cousin Pauline eyeing him off.
DOLLY: What? Are you sure?
GLADYS: Mum, are you sure?
ERROL: Are you really sure?
NAN DEAR: Yes! Yes! Of course I am. I can recognise a good man when I see one.

'Will I be handsome, will I be rich...?'

GLADYS *rolls her eyes, incredulous.* DOLLY *and* ERROL *hold each other's hands and look at each other adoringly.*

ERROL: Thank you, Mrs Dear, for your blessing, Mrs Dear.
NAN DEAR: It's 'Nan Dear' to you... son.

'I tell them tenderly...'

ERROL: Yes, Nan Dear.
DOLLY: And, Mum...?
GLADYS: Yes, Dolly?
DOLLY: It'll be all right.
GLADYS: You always say that.

A commotion is heard in the background.

DOLLY: It's Papa Dear! He's here! He's here!

The lights fade out on the 'Que Sera, Sera' chorus.

> *Que sera, sera,*
> *Whatever will be, will be,*
> *The future's not ours to see,*
> *Que sera, sera,*
> *What will be, will be,*
> *Que sera, sera...*

THE END

GLOSSARY

bodgies	boys who adopted certain fashions and behaviours during the 1950s
buka bung stew	stew made from nettles
goomees	drinkers
gubba	whitefella
humpy	a rough dwelling; a bush hut made from found materials
mamel	carpet snake
moom	bottom
widgies	female equivalent of the bodgies (see above)

Windmill Baby

David Milroy

David Milroy has written and directed a number of plays including *King Hit*, *Runumuk* and *Windmill Baby*, which won the 2004 Patrick White Award and the 2005 Equity Guild Award. David co-wrote and directed Sally Morgan's hit play *Cruel Wild Woman* and Barking Gecko's production of *Own Worst Enemy* for the Festival of Perth. He was Artistic Director of Yirra Yaakin Noongar Theatre for seven years and received a Myer Award in 2002 for his contribution to the development of Indigenous theatre. In 2000 David was a guest director of the American Playwrights' Conference in Connecticut and has attended the Australian National Playwrights' Conference on a number of occasions as a writer and director. David also directed *No Shame* (Mainstreet Theatre, Mt Gambier) and worked with Polyglot Theatre in Melbourne. He provided musical direction for *Sistergirl* and *Dead Heart* (Black Swan Theatre Company) and *Wild Cat Falling* (Perth Theatre Company). David currently lives in Perth and is actively involved in Native Title for his people, the Palyku of the Pilbara.

Rohanna Angus and Craig 'Chook' Pickett in the Yirra Yaakin production of WINDMILL BABY at the Subiaco Theatre, Perth, 2005. (Photo: Jon Green Photographer)

FIRST PERFORMANCE

Windmill Baby was first produced by Yirra Yaakin Theatre Company at the Subiaco Theatre Centre, Perth, on 23 February 2005, with the following cast:

    PERFORMER   Rohanna Angus

Director, David Milroy
Dramaturg, Irma Woods
Set and Lighting Designer, Alan Surgener
Costume Designer, Mand Markey
Musical Director, David Milroy
Musician, Craig 'Chook' Pickett

The production toured Australia between March and May 2006, was performed in the United Kingdom in June 2006, and in Canada and Ireland between September and November 2006, where the performer was Pauline Whyman and the musician Adam Fitzgerald.

AUTHOR'S NOTE

The first creative development for *Windmill Baby* was a week in Fitzroy Crossing. A week of sunny days and cold nights. I was accompanied by Alan Surgener the production designer and Kylie Farmer the project manager for Yirra Yaakin. Kylie was instructed to take notes because I have a bad habit of not writing anything down. 'Serge' was instructed to drive because I also have a bad habit of going through stop signs when I'm writing.

Creative developments are strange animals. They live in the physical and spiritual world. Sometimes you see them, sometimes you dream them and sometimes they can't be found anywhere. If the strange animals are around then a short walk down a dry river bed may be a ten-mile walk inside your head. A distant windmill on the landscape may be the one strange animal that haunts you into the writing process.

After the first couple of days, much to my relief, Kylie discarded the pen and pad, and Serge was still driving. I had promised my mother to visit some relatives of ours, so the next three days were spent going from one community to the next then back into town. My head filled with snippets of Toyota conversations and homestead history. The week came to an end and on our drive back to Broome we had to keep stopping because the strange animals were all over the road. The burnt-out boab tree, helicopter ringer, windmill, spinifex and all the conversations and characters past and present. I turned to Kylie in the back seat and asked if she still had the pen and pad.

KYLIE: Damn!

Fortunately my head had retained quite a deal more than usual and on my return to Sydney I burst into a fury of two-finger typing and the first draft of *Windmill Baby* was born. Fifteen or so drafts later and after much head-scratching, the play moved off the paper and onto the stage for the first time.

I'd especially like to thank the ANPC for their support and the Patrick White Award and Ningali Lawford Wolf for her input. I'd also like to thank the one person who won't let me get away with anything in my writing and that's Irma Woods, my dramaturg.

David Milroy

CHARACTERS

The play is written for one female actor, who plays the following characters and voices:

    OLD MAYMAY, elderly Aboriginal woman, seventies

    YOUNG MAYMAY, Aboriginal homestead laundry girl, late teens
    BOSS, boss of the station, early thirties
    WUNMAN'S MUM
    MALVERN, stockman, early twenties
    AUNTY DARBALLA, wise old Aboriginal woman, eighties
    SALLY, Aboriginal homestead cook, late teens
    MISSUS, the station boss's wife, early twenties
    WUNMAN, crippled Aboriginal gardener, early twenties
    BILLY GOGO, old Aboriginal wise man, eighties
    SKITCHIM, mongrel camp dog
    DR GILLESPIE, old white doctor

The play can be staged with a live solo guitarist also on stage, underscoring the action.

On stage is a rusted galvanised washtub and a dismantled push-pole clothes line.

A MUSICIAN *enters, sits and plays guitar.*

MAYMAY, *an old Aboriginal woman, enters, carrying a bag.*

As the song finishes, the light comes up. It's day.

OLD MAY: Oh my, fifty years has knocked the stuffing out of this old station. He look like graveyard. Graveyard full of memories. Like this old bed.

    MAYMAY *walks to an old rusty bed. She sits down, squeaking the rusty springs.*

Lot of bloody good memories from this one. Just like riding a bike. Funny thing that! My husband's name was Malvern, Malvern Starr. Awwww! Malvern did a lot of things on the station, he built that fence, he put that wire up for me…

    A mobile phone rings.

I'm not gonna worry about that. Aaargh!

    She answers the phone.

Hello, Maymay Starr speaking. Of course I'm all right! You only dropped me off five minutes ago. No, I told you I got some unfinished business here. You don't have to know everything. Stickybeak… Huh! I'm a proper bush blackfella, I know where to find water, all I have to do is look in my bag. Never you mind, now goodbye.

    She hangs up.

Hmmph! My daughter Gilly. Always checking up on me. Must think I got man out here or what…! Hmmph! I wish!

    She wanders over to the clothes line.

Now what was I saying…? My husband Malvern put this wire up for me. Strong enough to tether a bull. He cut this old clothes pole too. My old washtub.

    She walks over and peers inside the tub. She looks up with big surprised eyes.

For the past forty years I've had this feeling that I'd forgotten something. Now I know what it was—I forgot to hang out the missus' washing.

She lifts up a jowitch.

Well, if you start something you got to finish it. Even if it's not important any more. Now where's them dolly pegs?

She finds the peg bucket and hangs up the jowitch.

Poor missus. I used to think she was made out of wax. She had to keep out of the sun so she didn't melt. The day before she arrived on the station, boss had everyone raking the yard, oiling the boards and scrubbing the verandah. He came down to the camp barking like a dog after a dingo.

BOSS: And if one dog ain't tied up, I'll shoot the bloody lot.

OLD MAY: Had me beating the rugs.

BOSS: Harder, Maymay! Harder! She's got a dainty nose and I don't want it red from sneezing.

OLD MAY: Hmmph! Love does funny things to a man. The next day we seen the mail truck kicking up the dust. Malvern was a proper bush blackfella and hadn't seen many trucks before, so he grabbed a lasso in one hand, whip in the other, and hid behind the woodheap. The truck pulled up and there she sat. The little wax candle. No matter I whipped the rugs into butter, because all that sun and dust had made her nose as red as a beetroot. The missus weren't made for this country. But love does funny things to a woman.

She goes to go back to the washtub.

The sound of a windmill and creaking tin as the breeze picks up. The shadow of the windmill appears across the stage.

You hear that…? Listen. Wind picking up.
Who's there?
That you, Wunman…? Ruby?
Come on now, no good sneakin' up on an old woman.
Oh, it's you.
I ain't got time to talk now.
I got to finish the missus' washing.
Take a long time to dry 'em, fold 'em and put 'em away.

Ay, what's that?
No… I got no milk!
I'm an old woman now my gnangyas all dried up like figs.
No goat's milk either.
She finished long time ago.
You'd better go now.
Gotta get done before sundown.
I know I promised.
We'll have to cross it some other time.
Go on now.
You come back later.
Too much unfinished business around here.

The lights and the shadow and sound of the windmill fade.

A melon rolls onto the stage.

Ah! You checking up on me too, ay? One of Wunman's melons!

She picks up the melon.

Wunman got his name because he was one of two twin brothers. He came out first but, poor fella, he had a crippled-up arm like this, and a crippled-up leg. His brother came out second and was perfect but he took too long and was finished. Perfect but finished. In the old days a crippled baby would be left to die. Or if a gudiya had been sleeping with a black woman, gudiya and blackfella might say, 'Get rid of that baby!'

She holds the melon like a baby.

But his mummy held onto that little crippled-up Wunman and loved him like he was as perfect as Twoman. She didn't see no crippled-up arm or crippled-up leg. She looked at him and said…

WUNMAN'S MUM: You come out first so your name is Wunman and your brother come out last so his name is Twoman.

She walks to the bed and puts the melon down.

OLD MAY: The old gudiya boss treated us good. He wasn't worried about Wunman being a cripple, but the new boss had a cruel heart.

BOSS: I've got a station to run and I can't afford to feed blacks who can't earn their keep. Ship him out to the mission.

OLD MAY: Well, the new missus only ever talked in whispers but when she heard the boss talking bad way, that night she whispered at him awfully loud. The next morning he came shouting down the camp.
BOSS: Malvern! Malvern! Get out here!
OLD MAY: By jingos, Malvern thought he was gonna get a flogging so he grabbed a lasso in one hand, whip in the other, and hid under the bed.
BOSS: Maymay! Where's Malvern? If that lazy black bastard is still in bed—
YOUNG MAY: No, boss, he's not in bed. I saw him taking off with his whip and lasso.
BOSS: Hmmph! Then you'll do. I want you to find Wunman a job around the homestead and if he mucks up, the bloody Catholics can have him.
OLD MAY: Well, that scared the hell out of Wunman because he didn't know what a Catho-lick was.
YOUNG MAY: No worries, boss, he won't muck up.
OLD MAY: The boss walked off stamping his feet and Malvern shouted…
MALVERN: You bastard!
OLD MAY: And I shouted, 'Boss can't hear you from under the bed, Malvern'.
OLD MAY: First up I tried to teach him raking.
YOUNG MAY: Now, Wunman, you rake 'im this way and then you rake 'im that way and then you pick 'im up.
OLD MAY: Well, Wunman rake 'im this way and all the rubbish went that way, then his no-good leg give way and he fell over that way and I had to pick 'im up good way. Well, I was sitting there cracking my mooloo thinking about what to do with him when I heard the screen door open.
YOUNG MAY: No worries, missus. [*To* WUNMAN] Now, Wunman, listen up now. The missus said you gotta work in the vegie garden. Yui in the vegie garden. And she said you can use that goat cart. Yui the goat cart.

>*She stares for a while.*

And, Wunman, you better wear a jowitch in the vegie garden because when you crouch down like that I can see your boiled lollies. Wurrah.
OLD MAY: Well, Wunman like being the boss of the vegie garden, but he didn't like goats so he used to pull the cart himself. Like this…

Everyone started calling him Wungoat, 'til he started chucking rocks; no one called him Wungoat after that! Before he took over the garden everything would come up yellow. Even the kangaroos would be shaking their heads. [*Pause.*] But Wunman cleaned away the rubbish and filled the goat cart up with cow goona. For a whole week he worked day and night pushing that goona into the ground. Then he planted his seeds, looked at the windmill and went like this...

She twirls her gammy hand but nothing happens.

But nothing happened. So he did it a little harder...

She frowns at the windmill then twirls harder.

[*Smiling*] And that windmill started turning and the water started pumping and all them kangaroos started wagging their tails because everything started coming up green. The missus reckoned Wunman had green fingers. And she was right—very dark, green fingers.

The mobile phone rings.

Hello, Maymay Starr speaking. No, not lunchtime, suppertime. Anyway can't talk now, this thing's cooking my ear and I gotta finish hanging out the missus' washing... Yes, the missus' washing... No, I haven't got sunstroke! Goodbye!

She hangs up.

You know, my daughter bought me this for my birthday present, and I know she means well, but what I really wanted was the new 610 model that takes the photograph. You know!

She pretends to take photos, before placing the phone back in her bag.

I'm a pretty good-lookin' woman, hey. So you'd think that a good-lookin' woman, like me, would have a good-lookin' man. But nothing! Malvern was as ugly as a cowpad. But he did have a deadly mouth organ. And, you know, some people can pick up a musical instrument and play a song straight out. Well, Malvern wasn't one of those people. He had two notes... innnn...

The sound of a mouth organ sucking in...

And ouuuuttttt!

... and blowing out. This continues for some time.

Now, when I was a young heifer I didn't really care for mans. I was happy just doing my job. I'd have my soap and I'd be scrubbing and wringing and Malvern would be copying me on his blinkin' mouth organ. Iiiiin and oooooout.

She stares angrily as if looking at Malvern.

So I started off slow then a little bit faster and faster and faster and faster and faster and he kept playing faster and faster and I thought I could out-scrub him and he thought he could out-blow me. And I got wilder and wilder and he got puffier and puffier and then... That's it! I chucked the soap at him and knocked that hat clean off his head.

The mouth organ stops as MAYMAY *throws some soap. She stands staring in love lust towards the imaginary Malvern.*

I bin just fall in love with him then and there, because underneath that big hat was a... bald head. And a bald head can do strange things to a woman. But he weren't interested in me.

MALVERN: I'm a cleanskin. No woman gonna brand me.

OLD MAY: No matter, my branding iron was at Aunty Darballa's camp. She had all the love songs. But she didn't think too much of Malvern.

AUNTY DARBALLA: Aw, girl! You don't need a love song, you need something for your eyes, he proper ugly.

YOUNG MAY: But, Aunty, he's proper handsome from his eyebrows up.

AUNTY DARBALLA: Hmmph! Anyway, you're too late. Sally already been here for a song.

YOUNG MAY: [*screaming*] Sally? Sally! Sally! Sally! You stealing bugger!

SALLY: What you busting yourself for, Maymay?! I'm the one who should be angry. I know you been trying to steal my man. I seen you polishing his head. Innnnn! Ouuuutt! Innnnnn! Ouuutttt! Well, you can save your polishing for the kero lamp because he's my man, not yours. Anyway, there's a lot of other men bulling around here. Like... Wunman. He looks all right from back here... when the sun's going down... and he's not crouching.

YOUNG MAY: Now you listen here, Sally. Just because you been sneaking Malvern tucker don't make him yours. We're just gonna have to have a binyardi hit for hit.

OLD MAY: Just as I was lining up to knock Sally's gumbones down her big mouth, the missus came running up with her bible.

MISSUS: Girls! Girls! Girls! I don't want any fighting on the station. Now the good book tells us what we should do.

She pretends to open a bible and flick through.

Ah, here we go. We should cut Malvern in half and you can have half each.

OLD MAY: Well, we were both standing there with our mouths open when Sally said…

SALLY: I want the bottom half? Maymay, you can have his head.

YOUNG MAY: No, I don't want Malvern cut up so, Sally, you better have him.

MISSUS: Well, Maymay, I think that you truly love Malvern and you should have him.

OLD MAY: Suddenly Wunman looked pretty good to Sally.

SALLY: Wunman! You want a cup of tea?!

OLD MAY: After Malvern heard about me and Sally fighting over him he thought he was the world's greatest lover. But he was more like his mouth organ.

The mouth organ starts up again: iiin… ooout.

Now that I had my brand on Malvern, things were going well for us. The boss made him head stockman. The missus made Sally head of the household and Malvern made me pregnant.

The sound of a helicopter ringer approaching, kicking up dust, sheets blowing everywhere. MAYMAY *gets wild and abusive.*

Bugger off, you big dragonfly! I'm not a cow! You making the missus' washing dirty! Go on, get! Don't you poke your tongue at me!

The helicopter sound fades.

Bloody helicopter ringers. They run them cattle into the ground. Never mind the cow's in calf or the bullock's too old. Least in the old days we looked after them. I know 'cause I did a bit of droving myself. Malvern had to get a big mob of cattle to Derby but he was short a drover and a cook. His right-hand man Jim Jim had been horned by a bullock. Got him right in the guts. Malvern wanted to take him to the Native Hospital in Derby but the boss said…

BOSS: I can't spare any men. Maymay, you take his place.

MALVERN: She can't go, boss. She got a baby coming.

BOSS: Ah, I see! I made you head stockman and now you want to run the whole station?! Well, maybe you'd better keep your bloody mouth shut unless you want a taste of my whip.

OLD MAY: As the boss was walking off, Malvern reached under the seat of the dray and pulled out the thirty-thirty rifle.

YOUNG MAY: It's all right, Malvern. I've been droving before.

MALVERN: Not while you're carrying a baby.

YOUNG MAY: You gotta think of this one now…

MALVERN: I am thinking of the baby.

OLD MAY: He steadied himself… raised the rifle… took aim… and then… Whack!

WUNMAN: You tell Malvern I'm sorry for knockin' 'im out. Tell 'im I chuck the wood one way but he go the other way and hit 'im in the head.

OLD MAY: The next day Malvern swore Wunman up and down about chucking things. Wunman just crouched there looking at his toes and said nothing, but I knew he'd saved Malvern's life.

She sings a couple of lines from the Roy Rogers song, 'The Night Guard'.

Malvern was happiest when he was droving.

A couple more lines.

He used to sleep in the saddle of his night horse. If the cattle were unsettled it would shake its head and wake him up.

A couple more lines with a few changes of her own.

The first time I heard Malvern singing was to the cattle.

And a couple more of her own lines which she repeats.

Aww, boy! He couldn't sing for shit. But the cows liked it.

MALVERN: Now, Maymay, if it's a girl we'll call her your first name backwards, which would be 'Yamyam', and if it's a boy we'll call him my last name backwards which would be 'Rats'.

OLD MAY: I tell you what, we drove the cattle to Derby and he drove me crazy. [*Pause.*] After six weeks I was glad to get to Myall Bore about two mile from Derby. The biggest cattle trough in the world.

The boss had given Malvern three pounds for the run. He didn't really know what money was and I had to stop him from wiping his dhoomboo with it. [*Pause.*] We had a two-day wait for the ship to dock and another day for the ship to unload before we could move the cattle. So I thought three pounds, three days, let's go shopping!

YOUNG MAY: Here, Malvern, hold this material and smelly powder for the girls, and a big hanky for Aunty Darballa, and a big tin of boiled lollies for the kids, proper tobacco and pipe for you, and some seeds for Wunman—parsley, carrots, turnips and, look 'ere, flower seeds

MALVERN: Come on, Maymay, my arms are getting proper weak!

OLD MAY: Then I thought about all the times I'd been doing the washing, dreaming of owning a pair of lace jowitch just like the special ones the missus wore on Sundays. So I picked out the prettiest pair and put them right on the top of the pile in front of Malvern's face.

MALVERN: Wurrah!

OLD MAY: Well, next minute all my shopping was just floating in the air and Malvern took off like a wild bullock. The tin of boiled lollies busted all over the floor. Proper shame! So I picked everything up, paid for it and then went looking for that bald-headed bullock. By and by I found him sitting right in the middle of the jetty, sulking. I could see he had been spooked so I approached him downwind so he wouldn't stampede again.

MALVERN: Hmmph! You know, Maymay, you make me proper shame with that jowitch.

YOUNG MAY: Well, you make me proper shame dropping them boiled lollies all over the floor.

MALVERN: Hmmph! Who you buy them jowitch for anyway?

YOUNG MAY: I buy 'im, for you.

MALVERN: I'm not wearing no pretty jowitch!

YOUNG MAY: Don't be silly, I'm gonna wear 'im, but they're for you to look at.

MALVERN: Well, okay then, but only I gotta look at that pretty jowitch. You hide him in the saddlebag 'til we get back.

YOUNG MAY: [*with a wink*] No worries!

OLD MAY: Two days later we were all saddled up ready to head back to the station when Malvern made a quick dash back to Derby with a couple of killers to sell. He got the shopping bug and when he got back he give me a little box and inside was a pretty, shiny ring with a little red stone.

MALVERN: Maymay, that stone's a ruby and if our baby is a girl I don't wanna call her Yamyam, I wanna call her Ruby... Ruby Starr. And when she grows up you can give her that ring and tell her how she got her name.

OLD MAY: Ruby Starr. [*Pause.*] When we got back to the station them kids went crazy for those lollies! Little Jenny thought the lollies were too pretty to eat so she left hers in the sun. Took her two days to lick 'em off the fencepost. [*Pause.*] When I give Wunman his seeds he say...

WUNMAN: Thanks for the parsley and thanks for the turnips and thanks for the carrots.

OLD MAY: But when I gave him the flower seeds he dropped the parsley, turnips and carrots and run off to plant the flowers. He was that excited that he forgot about his no-good leg and he ran in a full circle before he got lined up straight and then... boooosh! Off he went to his garden by the windmill.

The windmill shadow appears again along with the sound of its creaking.

AUNTY DARBALLA:
Maymay, I seen Twoman in the garden.
Night-time I hear a stone on my roof.
I look out and see him talking to Wunman.
He missing his brother.
Wunman tell him, 'No, I got job to do'.
So Twoman is helping him.
He keep the maloo away from the flowers.
And he make the wind come.
That's a good place.
Lot of no-good around here but that's a happy place.
Proper happy place.

The windmill fades out.

OLD MAY: Every morning Wunman was supposed to take Sally the vegies. But he didn't like Sally, so after the boss rode off he'd take them to the missus instead. They'd sit on the verandah and he'd tell her silly stories about all the vegetables as if they were real people. Then he started taking her flowers as well.

YOUNG MAY: Hey, Wunman, you gonna make Sally jealous taking flowers to the missus all the time!

WUNMAN: Well, I don't like Sally. Her leg too skinny and her mouth too big.

YOUNG MAY: She been jealous for my baby… she want one too.

WUNMAN: You tell her I'm saving myself.

YOUNG MAY: Well, if I was you, Wunman, I wouldn't be too fussy.

MAYMAY addresses a woman in the front row of the audience.

OLD MAY: Eh, you wanna hear one of his silly stories? Come up here and sit with me… That's 'im.

The woman comes on stage and sits on a tin next to MAYMAY.

This is what he used to tell the missus! Now the potato grows under the ground and the pumpkin grows on top. And the pumpkin used to tease the potato because he was always covered in dirt. He'd say, 'Spud, spud, covered in mud, never wash 'til the river's in flood'. Well, potato used to get upset and he'd grow along under the ground trying to get away from pumpkin, but pumpkin would put out his vines and grow along on top of the ground teasing him all the time. 'Spud, spud, covered in mud, never wash 'til the river's in flood.' Anyways, one day just before the wet broke, there was a big lightning storm and all the cattle and horses stampeded through the station, smashed down the garden fence and squashed all the pumpkins. Then the rains came down and caused a big flood that washed all the mud away and all that was left sitting on the ground was this one washed potato. And then Wunman would get the missus to close her eyes. [*To the woman*] Close your eyes, and hold out her hand—hold out your hand.

The woman closes her eyes and MAYMAY *places the potato in the woman's hand.*

Open your eyes now. And he'd put it on her little wax palm and tell her, 'Even something that is covered in dirt and teased all its life can still be good and win in the end'. There, you like that potato story? That's not bad, hey? You got a story and a potato. So sit down now and stop being greedy. Eh, put that tin back…

The audience member goes back to her seat.

Well, one morning the boss forgot his tobacco and came riding back and caught Wunman sitting there talking pretty way to the missus. Only the house girls were allowed on the verandah, so his blood boiled over when he saw them. Next minute all hell broke loose. The boss grabbed Wunman by the scruff of the neck, dragged him off the verandah, threw him on the ground and gave him the flogging of his life. Made me proper sorry. I was supposed to be the boss for Wunman but I didn't know what to do any more, so I went and asked Billy Gogo. He was a wise old man. He knew which micky bull was gonna horn ya, which balls had to be cut and which goat ate the missus' washing.

YOUNG MAY: Now, old man, Wunman don't like Sally, but Sally like Wunman. The missus like Wunman and Wunman like the missus, but the boss don't like Wunman. So what I gotta do?

BILLY: Hmmm. Well, I don't blame him for not wanting Sally because her leg too skinny and her mouth too big. And I don't blame the boss for getting wild. Wunman shouldn't be on the verandah. Sound like Wunman need some company of his own. So what you gotta do is get him a dog.

OLD MAY: Haw, that Billy Gogo was a very wise man. The boss bought the missus a Frenchy poodle and I found Wunman a half-breed dingo—the front half was dingo and the back half was spotty dog. He called him Skitchim so that when he shouted, 'Skitchim!', all the dogs would run away except Skitchim. So he always got his feed first. But because the front half was dingo he started thinking about 'you know'. Mmm… that Skitchim he was a dog Casanova.

Skitchim appears.

At night Skitchim would come sneaking around the camp. He'd have a little sniff here.

She sniffs.

Nope! No lovin' here, and off he'd sneak to the next camp for another sniff.

She sniffs again.

Nope, no loving here either. Then he sniffed the air.

Three big sniffs.

Awwww, big mob of lovin' comin' from the missus' house. Then the screen door opened and there she stood, the little Frenchy poodle. Two months later the poodle had puppies. Their back half was poodle, the middle half was spotty dog and the front half was dingo.

MALVERN: Skitchim, you been no good knockin' up that poo dog. That boss tell me I gotta shoot you with this rifle. But I can't do that because you're Wunman's dog. So I'm sending you away. I want you to go bush and live with your other family, the dingos from your mother's side. So go now and don't come back to the station.

OLD MAY: So off went Skitchim to find his people. Poor fella. [*Pause*.] The day Skitchim busted up with Wunman, Wunman was back on the verandah talking to the missus as if Skitchim had meant nothing to him.

She picks up washing, goes to walk to the line, but drops it.

YOUNG MAY: Wunman! Wunman! Get Aunty Darballa for me… Quick! Hurry…! Hurry!

She walks painfully to the bed and sits.

AUNTY DARBALLA: Oh, Maymay, I'm proper sorry for you, girl, but your little baby come too soon. She finished. You lost a lot of blood so you sleep now. I've wrapped the baby for you and you can hold her tonight and maybe tomorrow we see how you feeling. Wunman's outside, he been worrying for you and wants to see you, I told him not to stay too long.

WUNMAN: You know, Maymay, sometimes bad things happen like what happened to my brother Twoman and to your little baby. But I know the old people are looking after them. This baby is special for you and Malvern so I came to ask if I could make a place for her in my garden. When Malvern gets back from the muster you can take him there and tell him that your baby is with the old people and she's resting in a happy place.

OLD MAY: All night I held my baby in my arms and in the morning I gave her to Wunman. I knew what he said was true. His garden was a happy place.

The sound fades as the lights brighten.

When I lost my little Ruby I also lost the ring that Malvern gave me. I had Wunman and the missus and Sally looking everywhere for it. I wanted to put it with my Ruby in the garden. [*She sighs.*] But never mind. [*Pause.*] Took me a while to come good. I was sad for a long time. Then one day the missus said she had something that would cheer me up. The mail truck had dropped off a box and inside was a vase for Wunman's flowers and a gramophone. She set it up on the step and invited me and Malvern to tea. True, ay! For blinkin' tea. Proper china teacup and saucer. Malvern didn't want to go. He blamed the boss for Ruby's death. But I told him, 'We're going for the missus, not the boss'. I got a bucket of water and scrubbed him all over. Up his nose, in his ears and under his arms. Every time he whinged, I scrubbed him harder. I borrowed the big hanky off Aunty Darballa and tied it round his neck, polished his head and cleaned his teeth with charcoal. I didn't have too much to make me pretty, but Wunman tied some flowers together and I stuck 'em in my hair. [*Pause.*] We all sat on the verandah drinking tea while Wunman cranked the gramophone on the steps.

She demonstrates Wunman cranking and looking at the record spinning.

He started getting dizzy from watching it spin around, so he had to crank 'im like this.

She demonstrates Wunman cranking while looking away.

MISSUS: So, Malvern, I hear that you are quite the musician with your mouth organ.

OLD MAY: If he said yes she might get him to play and that would be proper shame for all of us! But he did the right thing and told her a big lie.

MALVERN: No, 'e broke, missus. When I was cutting the balls off a bull he fell out my pocket into the tar. Now when I blow 'im he just go…

He makes a raspberry sound.

MISSUS: Oh, the poor mouth organ. And, Maymay, did Malvern buy you something nice in Derby?

YOUNG MAY: I got a Sunday jowitch just like you, missus, but only Malvern can look at 'im.

OLD MAY: Well, the boss got up with a 'Hmmph!', went into the store, and came back smelling like cake. [*Pause.*] After tea the missus wanted to have a dance. Malvern and the boss couldn't dance because their legs were like horseshoes. So Wunman cranked, Malvern chewed tobacco and the missus taught me how to dance. Malvern got so excited, he joined in with his mouth organ. Next minute Wunman got up and started dancing. It was a proper good party.

The sound of furniture being smashed, followed by a gunshot.

The lights snap to night-time.

BOSS: Mary, where the hell are ya! No good hiding from me, I'll find ya!

OLD MAY: No one knew where the missus was.

BOSS: I'll dance, if that'll make ya happy!

OLD MAY: He'd broken her vase and her heart all in the same day.

BOSS: I can buy you another vase, real pretty one, with horses on.

OLD MAY: Two pints of vanilla essence can do strange things to a man. The next minute the boss dragged Sally out of her camp. She was screaming and crying for him to let her go. But he was dragging her along by the arm and sayin' terrible things to her. This time Malvern grabbed his lasso in one hand, whip in the other, and fronted the boss.

MALVERN: You gone bloody crazy, boss. You let Sally go and give me the rifle.

BOSS: Ah, Mr Starr, the head stockman. You want the rifle, come and take it. Come on, Malvern, let's see how tough you are.

MALVERN: You put the rifle down and we'll sort this out. Man to man.

BOSS: I think I'll sort this out right now…

Boss aims his rifle but is distracted by something. Skitchim appears.

Skitchim… you mongrel bastard, you were supposed to be dead!

OLD MAY: The boss found a new target. Skitchim. He steadied himself… raised his rifle… took aim… and then… whack!

The lights come up.

WUNMAN: If the boss wake up, you tell 'im I chuck the wood one way but he go the other way and hit 'im in the head. And don't worry about the missus… she all right.

OLD MAY: The next day Malvern swore Skitchim up and down about coming back to the station, but I knew he'd saved Malvern's life.

She goes to move a drum and discovers some flowers underneath.

Ah, Wunman's flowers. Lot of people on the station named after flowers. There was Daisy, Rosy, Violet and Pansy. Yeah, Pansy, he was the best bronco buster. Malvern wasn't as romantic as Wunman, but he did give me flowers once… plain and self-raising. [*Pause.*] Wunman made the missus a new vase out of a pickled-onion jar and every day he'd leave fresh flowers for her, but she wouldn't come out and talk to anyone. Poor fella, he made me proper sorry. He had a no-good leg, a no-good arm and a no-good heart. [*Pause.*] Then he did something very cheeky. I was taking down the washing when he came up to the homestead pulling his billycart full of potatoes.

YOUNG MAY: Hey, Wunman! What the blinkin' hell you doing with all them potato?

WUNMAN: They for the missus.

YOUNG MAY: Hmmph! They'll go rotten on the verandah just like the flowers.

WUNMAN: I'm not gonna leave 'em on the verandah.

YOUNG MAY: Where you gonna put 'em?

WUNMAN: I'm not gonna put 'em anywhere, I'm gonna chuck 'em!

YOUNG MAY: Awww, Wunman! You got to get over this chuckin' business.

OLD MAY: Next minute he pick 'im up like this. And chuck him straight through the missus' window. Then another and another and he kept chucking, bullseye each time.

YOUNG MAY: Wunman, you gone blinkin' crazy! If the boss finds out he'll whip you all the way to the mission.

WUNMAN: Boss the crazy one! He like that pumpkin, one day he'll get what's coming to him.

OLD MAY: Well, after Wunman had chucked all his potatoes he just sat there staring at the homestead. Then, just as I was gonna drag him away, she came out onto the verandah and held his hands with the little potato inside. I thought this is no good… but potatoes can do strange things to a woman.

The shadow and sound of the creaking windmill return.

AUNTY DARBALLA:
I seen a little baby playing by the windmill.
He proper cheeky too!
When he see me, he hide behind the windmill.
I call him Windmill Baby.

Maybe the missus gonna have that Windmill Baby.
Could be after all that dancing she been doing.
Gonna be a big baby.
He always hungry.
[*Chuckling*] Always hungry for milk.

The windmill sound fades.

OLD MAY: The missus started getting sick in the morning and when she told the boss she was pregnant they had the biggest row. He didn't want a baby but she did.

MISSUS: Maymay, I want you to help me make a quilt for my baby.

OLD MAY: She opened up the suitcase and we looked through all the pretty cloth she had brought up from Perth. There was satin, lace, velvet, silk and lots of pretty patterns. We chose pink tea roses and dancing fairies. As she finished each patch I'd stuff it with a little bit of lamb's wool to make 'im soft and warm.

MISSUS: Maymay, when this baby is old enough I'll show him the quilt and I'll tell him, 'Once upon a time the fairies lived in Wunman's garden amongst the flowers and they asked Mummy to show them how to dance. So Wunman cranked the gramophone and I taught them how to waltz. When the fairies could dance they put on a big party and danced around the pretty ring with the ruby stone.' [*Pause.*] Maymay, I want you to forget about the quilt tomorrow and see if you can catch me some fish down the river.

YOUNG MAY: But you don't like fish, missus.

MISSUS: Um… it will be good for baby's bones.

OLD MAY: The missus wasn't a very good liar. So the next morning I told Wunman…

YOUNG MAY: You stay in your garden and no more humbugging the missus, she needs her rest. And if the missus talk to you, just tell her you got no more stories and you're too busy to talk.

OLD MAY: Then off I went, but I gave 'em a good herding look before I left. When I got back, wurrah!

YOUNG MAY: Wunman, you stop cranking that gramophone and get off the verandah! And, missus, you shouldn't be dancing like that with that baby in your belly!

OLD MAY: Well, they both give me a herding look straight back. If a bull wants to jump a fence and a cow is in calf, you just gotta let 'em be. [*Pause.*] That wasn't the only thing going wrong on the station; we were in the middle of a drought. There was water in the bores but the country had dried up and there was no feed for the cattle. So the boss started taking it out on his men. Freddy Cole got horsewhipped and ran away, but the policemans brought him back. The next time he ran away, gudiyas came in from other stations and met with the boss.

The lights fade to night-time.

They talked long into the night. We knew something was up so we stayed close to camp. [*Pause.*] When Malvern came home he looked proper worried. He told me to bring Wunman to our camp.

MALVERN: Now, Wunman, you gotta listen to me now. Tomorrow they're going out looking for Freddy Cole and if they find him he'll get a bullet. There's been a lot of bad yarns going around so I want you to come to Derby with me and the boss before that Windmill Baby is born. You can cross the river to the mission from there… You don't come, you'll get a bullet like poor runaway fella gonna get. Pack what you need. We leave at sun-up.

OLD MAY: That night I sat with Wunman in his garden for one last time.

WUNMAN: You know, Maymay, the missus read to me about Eden. She tell me my garden is just like that one. Everything comes up green and it's a proper happy place. [*Pause.*] And you know, there was two fellas who loved each other but things went wrong for them because they broke the law. Maybe one was black and maybe one was white. What colour love, Maymay? Maybe the colour of rainwater or red like that pretty ring you lost. But I don't think it's just black and I don't think it's just white. [*Pause.*] Malvern tell me I got to cross that river. I know that's what I gotta do. Before I go, I want you to promise me that one day you'll bring that Windmill Baby to me. Make sure you keep that promise, Maymay. Make sure you keep that promise.

OLD MAY: That night Wunman stayed in his garden, talking to his twin brother Twoman, and telling his stories. At sun-up we… [*sighing*] found him dead. [*Pause.*] Dr Gillespie came to keep an eye on the missus. He'd been in the war and a big bomb had gone off and knocked some metal into his leg. It must have been forty years before I seen a man with a good pair of legs. The wet broke early that year and ended the drought. And that wasn't the only thing that caught us by surprise.

DOCTOR: Maymay! Her waters have broken. I'm going to need a hand in here.

OLD MAY: Two wets in one day! [*Pause.*] Well, giving birth is the one thing that womans know how to do naturally. Just like shopping! And just like shopping, man gotta keep his mouth shut.

YOUNG MAY: Come on now, missus, you can do it. Big push now. That's him, keep 'im comin'. That's 'im. Big breath. One more now. He comin' now. Come on, big push, big push. That's it, here he comes. Big push, nearly there, last push. *Yay!*

OLD MAY: Just like bettin' on horses.

DOCTOR: Maymay, take the baby into the kitchen and count his fingers and toes. I'll be in there directly.

OLD MAY: I counted his fingers like in the stockyard.

YOUNG MAY: One, two, three, four, five. Cross biggest mob of fingers and toes!

OLD MAY: When the doctor came in he unwrapped him… and then wrapped him straight back up again.

YOUNG MAY: You gonna wash him, doctor?

DOCTOR: Bring him outside. Now, I want you to get rid of the baby. Get rid of it. It's not a white baby. Do you understand what I'm saying? Get rid of it before the boss gets back. Only you and me have to know. Tell everyone its heart gave out just after he was born. And I'll tell the missus.

Pause.

YOUNG MAY: Baby, you got your pretty quilt… so you come back to my camp and we'll think of something to do.

She rocks back and forth with the baby.

I know you hungry, but don't cry… I'll get a goat and you can have the biggest mob of warm milk. In the morning I'll take you back to the missus and tell her everything is all right. Your baby not finished. He just with Aunty Maymay for a while so you could sleep… so you could sleep.

OLD MAY: In the morning I took the baby back to the house.
No music.
No flowers.

The windmill was still.
The happiness had gone.

YOUNG MAY: Now, baby, most of the mob have gone bush for the wet, but if we can cross the river, maybe they can take you into the desert or to a mission. It's a two-day walk to the crossing so we have to make good time before it's flooded over. You gotta be good now for your aunty.

OLD MAY: I walked all day watching the clouds building in the sky. That night we slept inside a burnt-out boab tree and then headed off at sun-up. We made the crossing by sundown.

The lights come up on a Kimberley sunset.

Red sky.
Red water.
Fallen banks.
Broken branches.
The river was in flood.

Thunder and lightning. A flood.

YOUNG MAY: Now, Windmill Baby, we gonna try and cross this river now and I don't want you to cry… your mummy wouldn't want you to cry… your mummy's a good woman. She taught me how to sew, we made this quilt together… Here we go now… Once upon a time the fairies lived in Wunman's garden amongst the flowers…

OLD MAY: I could smell the baby's breath on my shoulder.

YOUNG MAY: They asked Mummy to show them how to dance…

OLD MAY: His feet were as soft as a lamb.

YOUNG MAY: So Wunman cranked the gramophone and your mummy taught them how to waltz…

OLD MAY: His little hand gripped my finger.

YOUNG MAY: They put on a big party and danced around the pretty ring with the ruby stone.

OLD MAY: In the swirling darkness the river took him from my arms.

The sunset fades and the lights brighten.

The phone rings.

Hello, Maymay Starr speaking. Yui. My business just about finished. No, I don't want to get picked up by Cousin Freddy's helicopter. Bring the Toyota. See you!

She hangs up.

There! The missus' washing is just about dry now. [*Pause.*] Time to finish this business.

She collects the flowers, places them down and arranges them.

Ruby, I had to leave this station and there's a lot that I never got to tell you. Your daddy passed on now but I want you to know he was a good man and a good stockman and it was him that give you your name from that ruby stone. That ring is long gone. I know a lot of years have passed but I never stopped thinking about you and I've always loved you. [*Pause.*] Now, Wunman, I know you couldn't go to the mission and I know you couldn't stay on the station but when you left, a lot of goodness went with you… I want you to know that when that Windmill Baby came I also had nowhere to go. I had no choice either… I wish things could have been different. I'm sorry.

She takes a quilt from her bag and holds it.

The shadow of the windmill.

She stares at the windmill.

Windmill Baby, we never got across that river but I did my best. I haven't got much to give you now but here's that quilt me and your mummy made for you… I never got to keep my promise to your daddy… but maybe he come for you tonight… and he can tell you that story… you know that potato one. [*She puts the quilt down. Pause.*] How you end that story?

THE END

GLOSSARY

binyardi	fight, to fight
boab tree	found in the North-Kimberley region of Western Australia
cow goona	cow poo
dhoomboo	bottom
gnangyas	breasts
gudiya	white person
gumbones	teeth
jowitch	knickers
love songs	traditional song thought to lure a male/female
maloo	kangaroo, big male
mooloo	head lice
smelling like cake	drinking vanilla essence, which was the liquor to have when you had no liquor
wurrah	shame, said when embarrassed or shocked
yui	yes

www.currency.com.au

Visit Currency Press' website now to:

- Buy your books online
- Browse through our full list of titles, from plays to screenplays, books on theatre, film and music, and more
- Choose a play for your school or amateur performance group by cast size and gender
- Obtain information about performance rights
- Find out about theatre productions and other performing arts news across Australia
- For students, read our study guides
- For teachers, access syllabus and other relevant information
- Sign up for our email newsletter

The performing arts publisher

www.ingramcontent.com/pod-product-compliance
Lightning Source LLC
Chambersburg PA
CBHW040305170426
43194CB00022B/2909